Preface

This book is designed to be your comprehensive companion in your journey to becoming proficient in Microsoft SQL Server Text Book. Whether you are a beginner taking your first steps into the world of SQL databases or an experienced database professional seeking to deepen your knowledge, this book has something to offer you.

In today's data-driven world, the importance of managing data efficiently cannot be overstated. Microsoft SQL Server, a robust and versatile database management system, is at the heart of countless applications, powering businesses, industries, and organizations of all sizes. With its rich feature set, scalability, and integration capabilities, SQL Server has become an indispensable tool for database professionals, developers, and administrators.

In "Mastering Microsoft SQL," we have carefully curated a wealth of knowledge, practical insights, and hands-on examples to guide you through the complexities of SQL Server. From understanding the fundamentals of SQL to mastering advanced database administration techniques, this book is structured to help you build a strong foundation and progress to expert-level skills.

Throughout these pages, you will find:

Clear Explanations: We strive to make complex concepts accessible by providing clear and concise explanations.

Practical Examples: Real-world scenarios and practical examples illustrate how SQL Server is used in different contexts.

Step-by-Step Tutorials: Detailed, step-by-step tutorials guide you through essential tasks and operations.

Best Practices: We emphasize best practices for database design, development, and administration.

Advanced Topics: Dive into advanced topics such as performance tuning, high availability, and cloud integration to enhance your skills.

Whether you are studying this book as part of your formal education, using it for professional development, or simply exploring SQL Server out of curiosity, we hope you find it both informative and engaging.

We would like to express our gratitude to the SQL Server community, whose collective knowledge and passion for databases have contributed to the content of this book. Additionally, we acknowledge the support of our families, friends, and colleagues who have been a constant source of encouragement and inspiration.

This book is designed to be accessible to readers with varying levels of expertise. Each chapter builds upon the previous one, but feel free to skip around based on your interests and needs. Whether you're looking for practical tutorials, theoretical insights, or real-world examples, you'll find them here.

We encourage you to engage with the material actively. Practice with hands-on exercises, experiment with database systems, and apply what you learn to your own projects. The knowledge you gain from this book will empower you to tackle real-world data management challenges with confidence.

Chapter 1: Introduction to Microsoft SQL Server

1.1 History and Evolution

Microsoft SQL Server is a relational database management system (RDBMS) developed by Microsoft. Since its inception, it has undergone significant changes and improvements. Here is an overview of its history and evolution:

SQL Server 1.0 (1989):

Microsoft SQL Server's journey began with its first release in 1989. SQL Server 1.0 was originally developed by Sybase and was a joint project between Microsoft and Sybase. It was designed for OS/2, a 16-bit operating system. The first version laid the foundation for future database systems.

SQL Server 4.2 (1992):

SQL Server 4.2 was a significant release, marking Microsoft's full control over its development. It introduced support for Windows NT, Microsoft's new 32-bit operating system. This version established SQL Server as a competitive RDBMS in the enterprise space.

SQL Server 6.0 (1995):

SQL Server 6.0 brought major improvements, including support for distributed queries, triggers, and stored procedures. It enhanced performance and scalability. SQL Server 6.0 established Microsoft's commitment to the enterprise database market.

SQL Server 7.0 (1998):

SQL Server 7.0 introduced a complete rewrite of the database engine. It included significant performance enhancements, support for OLAP (Online Analytical Processing), and data warehousing. SQL Server 7.0 marked the beginning of Microsoft's leadership in the database market.

SQL Server 2000 (2000):

SQL Server 2000 continued to build on the success of its predecessor. It introduced features like the Analysis Services for OLAP, Data Transformation Services (DTS), and support for XML. SQL Server 2000 improved scalability and business intelligence capabilities.

SQL Server 2005 (2005):

SQL Server 2005 brought a significant overhaul, introducing the .NET Framework integration and the Common Language Runtime (CLR). It introduced the SQL Server Management Studio (SSMS) and enhanced reporting and analysis capabilities with SQL Server Reporting Services (SSRS) and SQL Server Analysis Services (SSAS).

SQL Server 2008 (2008):

SQL Server 2008 introduced features such as transparent data encryption, policy-based management, and support for spatial data. It emphasized performance improvements and better support for large-scale data.

SQL Server 2012 (2012):

SQL Server 2012 focused on improved business intelligence tools and capabilities. It introduced the Power View feature for data visualization and enhanced support for column store indexes.

SQL Server 2014 (2014):

SQL Server 2014 introduced In-Memory OLTP, a feature designed to accelerate transaction processing. It also enhanced disaster recovery options with the addition of Always On Availability Groups.

SQL Server 2016 (2016):

SQL Server 2016 introduced numerous enhancements, including support for JSON, improved security features, and the integration of R for advanced analytics. It also introduced Polybasic, which allows for querying data in Hadoop and Azure blob storage.

SQL Server 2017 (2017):

SQL Server 2017 extended its platform to Linux, making it available on both Windows and Linux operating systems. It improved support for graph data processing and introduced Adaptive Query Processing for query optimization.

SQL Server 2019 (2019):

SQL Server 2019 introduced Big Data Clusters, enabling the integration of big data and relational data into a single platform. It enhanced support for containers and Kubernetes, making it more cloud-friendly. The release continued to focus on advanced analytics and AI integration.

SQL Server 2022 (2022):

SQL Server 2022 Developer is a full-featured free edition, licensed for use as a development and test database in a non-production environment.

SQL Server continues to evolve with each new version, adapting to the changing needs of enterprises and the technology landscape. It remains a critical part of Microsoft's data platform, offering a wide range of features and capabilities for data management, business intelligence, and data analytics.

1.2 Editions and Versions

Microsoft SQL Server is a powerful relational database management system (RDBMS) with various editions and versions catering to different user needs and scenarios. Below, I provide details about some of the editions and versions of Microsoft SQL Server:

SQL Server Editions:

SQL Server Express Edition: SQL Server Express is a free, lightweight version of SQL Server. It is suitable for small-scale applications, individual developers, and learning purposes.

Key Features:

Limited to 1 CPU and 1 GB of RAM.

Database size is limited to 10 GB per database.

Supports basic database functionality and tools.

Use Cases: Small desktop applications, lightweight web applications, learning, and development.

SQL Server Standard Edition: SQL Server Standard is a mid-tier edition designed for medium-sized organizations. It offers more features and scalability compared to Express.

Key Features:

Supports up to 24 cores and 128 GB of RAM.

Includes advanced features like basic reporting, analytics, and high availability.

Use Cases: Medium-sized businesses, departmental databases, web applications.

SQL Server Enterprise Edition: Description: SQL Server Enterprise is the top-tier edition with advanced features, scalability, and performance enhancements. It's designed for mission-critical and large-scale applications.

Key Features:

Supports up to 640 logical processors and 12 TB of RAM.

Includes advanced features like Always On Availability Groups, online operations, and advanced security.

Use Cases: Large enterprises, critical applications, high-demand databases.

SQL Server Developer Edition: SQL Server Developer Edition offers the same features as the Enterprise Edition but is intended for development and testing purposes. It has all Enterprise features but is not licensed for production use.

Key Features:

Ideal for developing and testing applications.

Includes all Enterprise features for development and experimentation.

Use Cases: Development and testing environments, building and testing applications.

SQL Server Versions:

SQL Server also has multiple versions, each with its own features and enhancements. Some notable versions include:

SQL Server 2022: SQL Server 2022 Developer is a full-featured free edition, licensed for use as a development and test database in a non-production environment.

SQL Server 2019: SQL Server 2019 introduced features like Big Data Clusters, which enable data virtualization and analysis across structured and unstructured data sources.

Key Features: Big Data Clusters, enhanced security features, improved query performance.

SQL Server 2017: SQL Server 2017 focused on cross-platform compatibility, with support for Linux. It also introduced graph database capabilities.

Key Features: Linux support, graph database support, enhanced performance.

SQL Server 2016: Description: SQL Server 2016 brought improvements in data encryption, in-memory processing, and JSON support.

Key Features: Always Encrypted, In-Memory OLTP enhancements, JSON support.

These editions and versions of Microsoft SQL Server offer a range of features and scalability options to meet diverse database requirements. The choice of edition and version depends on factors like the size of the organization, the scale of the application, and the specific features needed for a particular use case. It's essential to carefully evaluate your requirements to select the most suitable edition and version for your database needs.

1.3 Architecture and Components

Microsoft SQL Server has a robust and scalable architecture composed of various components that work together to manage and process data efficiently. Below, I provide an overview of the architecture and key components of Microsoft SQL Server:

Database Engine: The Database Engine is the core component responsible for storing, processing, and securing data in SQL Server. It includes several subcomponents:

Relational Engine: This component manages SQL queries, transaction processing, and data storage. It interprets and optimizes SQL queries for data retrieval and modification.

Storage Engine: Responsible for physical data storage, data retrieval, and caching. It manages the storage of data in data files and transaction logs.

SQL Server Instances: An instance represents an installation of SQL Server on a computer. Multiple instances can coexist on a single server, each operating independently with its own databases, security, and configurations.

Databases: Databases are containers that store data, schemas, tables, and other database objects. SQL Server supports multiple databases within a single instance.

Query Processor: The Query Processor is responsible for parsing, optimizing, and executing SQL queries. It includes components such as the Query Optimizer, which determines the most efficient execution plan for a query.

Buffer Manager: The Buffer Manager is responsible for managing data pages in memory. It caches frequently accessed data pages to improve query performance.

Transaction Manager: The Transaction Manager ensures the integrity of transactions within the database. It manages the ACID (Atomicity, Consistency, Isolation, Durability) properties of transactions.

Lock Manager: The Lock Manager controls access to data by managing locks on data resources. It enforces concurrency control to ensure data consistency in multi-user environments.

Lock Manager: The Lock Manager controls access to data by managing locks on data resources. It enforces concurrency control to ensure data consistency in multi-user environments.

Services: SQL Server services are processes responsible for managing various aspects of SQL Server functionality. Key services include the Database Engine service, SQL Server Agent service for scheduling tasks, and the Full-Text Search service for text-based searching.

Data Access APIs: SQL Server provides various APIs and protocols for connecting to and interacting with the database. Common APIs include ADO.NET, ODBC, JDBC, and the T-SQL language for querying and managing data.

Tools and Utilities: SQL Server includes a suite of tools and utilities for database administration, development, and monitoring. These tools include SQL Server Management Studio (SSMS), SQL Server Data Tools (SSDT), and SQL Server Profiler for performance tuning.

Reporting and Analysis Services: SQL Server offers Reporting Services (SSRS) for creating, managing, and delivering reports, as well as Analysis Services (SSAS) for data analysis and multidimensional modelling.

High Availability and Replication: SQL Server provides features for high availability, such as Always on Availability Groups and failover clustering. It also supports replication for distributing data across multiple servers.

Integration Services: SQL Server Integration Services (SSIS) is a platform for building data integration and ETL (Extract, Transform, Load) solutions.

SQL Server's architecture is designed to be scalable, reliable, and flexible, making it suitable for a wide range of data management scenarios, from small businesses to large enterprises.

1.4 Licensing and Installation

Microsoft SQL Server offers various licensing models to cater to different organizational needs and budgets. Licensing considerations are crucial when planning to install and use SQL Server. Here are some key aspects of licensing:

Edition Selection: Choose the appropriate SQL Server edition (e.g., Express, Standard, Enterprise) based on your organization's requirements. Each edition has different features and licensing costs.

Licensing Models: Per-Core Licensing: In this model, you need to purchase a license for each physical or virtual core in the server running SQL Server. This model provides scalability and flexibility.

Server + CAL (Client Access License) Licensing: With this model, you license the SQL Server software for a specific server, and then you need CALs for each user or device accessing the server. CALs are required for client applications that directly connect to the SQL Server.

Software Assurance: Consider purchasing Software Assurance with your SQL Server licenses. It offers benefits like version upgrades, support, and flexibility in license reassignment.

Virtualization: If you plan to run SQL Server in virtualized environments, understand the licensing implications. Microsoft's virtualization licensing rules can be complex.

Developer and Test Licensing: SQL Server Developer Edition is available for development and testing purposes at a lower cost. Be aware of the licensing restrictions for this edition, which prohibits production use.
License Compliance: Ensure compliance with licensing agreements. Microsoft conducts license audits, so it's important to keep accurate records of your licenses.
Installing Microsoft SQL Server:
Installing SQL Server involves several steps, and the specific process can vary depending on the edition and version you are using. Here's a general overview of the installation process:
System Requirements: Before installation, ensure that your server or workstation meets the hardware and software requirements specified for the SQL Server edition and version you plan to install.
Installation Media: Obtain the installation media, which can be a physical DVD or downloadable ISO image from Microsoft's website.
Installation Wizard: Run the SQL Server Installation Wizard. It will guide you through the installation process.
Edition and Features: Select the SQL Server edition and features you want to install. Some editions offer additional features like Reporting Services, Analysis Services, and Integration Services, which can be selected during installation.
Instance Configuration: Choose whether to install a default or named instance of SQL Server. A default instance uses the server's name, while a named instance can have a custom name.
Server Configuration: Configure SQL Server service accounts, authentication mode (Windows or mixed mode), and specify SQL Server administrators (sysadmins).
Database Engine Configuration: Configure options like data directories, collation settings, and specify additional features like Full-Text Search.
Installation Progress: Review your selections and start the installation. The progress will be displayed, and you may need to perform additional tasks if required.
Post-Installation Configuration: After installation, configure additional settings, such as setting up maintenance plans, configuring security, and applying service packs and updates.
Testing and Verification: Verify that SQL Server is running as expected and test database connectivity.
Remember to follow best practices for security, backup, and maintenance after installation to ensure the health and performance of your SQL Server instance.

1.5 **Exercise**

Exercise 1 – MCQ

1. What year marked the initial release of Microsoft SQL Server?
A. 1989
B. 1995
C. 2000
D. 2005
2. Which edition of Microsoft SQL Server is primarily designed for enterprise-level applications and data warehousing?
A. Express Edition
B. Standard Edition
C. Enterprise Edition
D. Developer Edition
3. The core components of SQL Server's architecture include:
A. Query Optimizer, Buffer Manager, and Lock Manager
B. Service Broker, Integration Services, and Analysis Services
C. Resource Governor, Full-Text Search, and Database Mail
D. SQL Agent, Extended Events, and Distributed Replay
4. What is the primary licensing model used for SQL Server Enterprise Edition?
A. Per User
B. Per Core
C. Per Server
D. Per Instance
5. Which of the following versions of SQL Server introduced the concept of In-Memory OLTP (Online Transaction Processing)?
A. SQL Server 2005

B. SQL Server 2012
C. SQL Server 2014
D. SQL Server 2019
6. SQL Server Express Edition has limitations on:
A. Database size and maximum memory utilized
B. Number of concurrent connections and supported languages
C. CPU usage and available disk space
D. Supported data types and query complexity
7. The main components of SQL Server's installation include:
A. Database Engine, SQL Agent, and Management Studio
B. Integration Services, Reporting Services, and Analysis Services
C. Full-Text Search, Service Broker, and Replication
D. Resource Governor, Query Store, and Extended Events
8. Which SQL Server edition is provided for development and testing purposes but has the same features as the Enterprise Edition?
A. Standard Edition
B. Express Edition
C. Developer Edition
D. Web Edition
9. SQL Server's Buffer Pool is responsible for:
A. Caching data and indexes in memory
B. Executing query plans and optimizing queries
C. Managing concurrent user connections
D. Scheduling jobs and tasks
10. SQL Server's licensing model based on the number of physical processors or virtual cores is most applicable to:
A. Standard Edition
B. Enterprise Edition
C. Developer Edition
D. Express Edition

Exercise 2 – True/False

1. Microsoft SQL Server was initially developed by Oracle Corporation.
2. SQL Server Express is a full-featured free edition of SQL Server, limited by resource usage and database size.
3. SQL Server uses a single-tier architecture for handling database operations.
4. SQL Server offers a free version without any limitations on database size or resource usage.
5. The first version of SQL Server was released in the 1990s.
6. SQL Server Enterprise Edition includes all features available in the Standard Edition.
7. The SQL Server Database Engine manages data storage, processing, and security.
8. SQL Server follows a per-user licensing model, where the number of users accessing the database does not affect the licensing cost.
9. SQL Server initially ran exclusively on Windows-based platforms.
10. SQL Server Developer Edition is limited in terms of features compared to the Standard Edition.

Exercise 3 – Fill in the blanks

1. Microsoft SQL Server was first introduced in the year ___________.
2. The initial version of SQL Server was primarily based on the technology acquired from ___________.
3. Over the years, SQL Server has undergone significant enhancements, with milestone developments such as the introduction of ___________ in [year].
4. The evolution of SQL Server reflects a shift towards increased focus on ___________ and improved ___________.
5. The different editions of SQL Server include ___________, ___________, and ___________.
6. SQL Server Express is known for its ___________ and is suitable for small-scale applications with limited ___________.
7. The latest version of SQL Server as of [current year] is ___________.
8. The architecture of SQL Server primarily consists of the ___________, ___________, and ___________.
9. The core components of SQL Server include the ___________ responsible for query processing and optimization.

10. SQL Server's architecture emphasizes the use of ___________ to enhance performance and scalability.

Exercise 4 – One word answer

1. What company developed SQL Server?
2. Which version introduced Always On availability groups?
3. Name one SQL Server edition designed for small businesses.
4. What component handles query optimization?
5. What determines SQL Server licensing cost?
6. What part manages storage in SQL Server?
7. What governs the number of SQL Server instances?
8. Which SQL Server component ensures data durability?
9. What's the SQL Server Express installation size limit?
10. What's the primary function of the SQL Server Agent?

Exercise 5 – Small answer

1. When was the first version of Microsoft SQL Server released?
2. Which company originally developed SQL Server before Microsoft acquired it?
3. Name one significant milestone in the evolution of SQL Server.
4. How many editions of SQL Server are typically available?
5. What distinguishes the Enterprise Edition from the Standard Edition?
6. Name two recent versions of SQL Server and highlight a major feature introduced in each.
7. What are the main components of the SQL Server Database Engine?
8. What role does the SQL Server Agent play in the architecture?
9. Explain the purpose of the Buffer Pool in SQL Server.
10. What are the different licensing models available for SQL Server?

Exercise 6 – Long answer

1. Explain the key milestones in the evolution of Microsoft SQL Server from its inception to its current version, highlighting significant enhancements or changes in each major release.
2. Discuss the pivotal role of the partnership between Microsoft and Sybase in the creation of the initial versions of SQL Server and how the subsequent divergence shaped its evolution.
3. Compare and contrast the features and limitations of SQL Server editions such as Enterprise, Standard, and Express, emphasizing their suitability for different business environments.
4. Detail the advancements and key differences between major versions of SQL Server (e.g., 2008, 2012, 2016, 2019), focusing on technological breakthroughs, performance improvements, and new functionalities introduced in each version.
5. Describe the core architectural components of SQL Server, including the Database Engine, SSIS (SQL Server Integration Services), SSAS (SQL Server Analysis Services), and SSRS (SQL Server Reporting Services), highlighting their roles in the SQL Server ecosystem.
6. Provide a step-by-step guide detailing the installation process for SQL Server, including prerequisites, configuration options, best practices, and considerations for various deployment types (e.g., standalone, clustered).
7. Elaborate on SQL Server's scalability options, discussing techniques such as partitioning, sharding, and replication, and their applicability in handling large volumes of data or high transaction rates.
8. Evaluate the different high availability solutions offered by SQL Server, such as Always On Availability Groups, Failover Clustering, and Log Shipping, emphasizing their benefits, trade-offs, and implementation considerations.
9. Outline the various licensing models available for SQL Server, discussing their complexities and implications for different organizational structures or deployment scenarios.
10. Explain the underlying architecture and mechanisms of SQL Server's query processing, discussing query optimization, execution plans, and the factors influencing query performance.

Answer

Exercise 1:

Answer: 1: A, 2: C, 3: A, 4: B, 5: C, 6: A, 7: A, 8: C, 9: A, 10: B

Exercise 2:

Answer: 1: False, 2: True, 3: False, 4: False, 5: True, 6: False, 7: True, 8: False, 9: True, 10: False

Exercise 3:

Answer: 1: 1989, 2: Sybase, 3: 2004, 4: cloud integration, data analytics, 5: Enterprise, Standard, and Express, 6: lightweight nature, resources, 7: Licensing, 9: Query Optimizer, 10: in-memory technologies

Online Resources

Introduction to Microsoft SQL Server: https://youtu.be/ea8J7PsfaEc
Introduction to DBMS: https://youtu.be/SwB6RTAQ-o0
MySQL – Quick Introduction: https://youtu.be/-7NohrJoDko
Database Management System (DBMS): https://youtu.be/0giJSc9vBKU

ONLINE RESOURCES

Practice Paper
Link: https://forms.office.com/r/F7tkB8vLap
QR Code:

Video Content
Link: https://www.youtube.com/playlist?list=PLzlh_31VWEFpnGVgZ2R9XA1_xdhGtxaHY
QR Code:

Chapter 2 : Getting Started with SQL

2.1 SQL Basics

SQL (Structured Query Language) is a standardized programming language used to manage and manipulate relational databases, including Microsoft SQL Server. SQL basics involve understanding the fundamental commands and syntax used to interact with databases. Here are some essential SQL basics for Microsoft SQL Server:

SELECT Statement:

The SELECT statement retrieves data from one or more tables. It is the primary command for querying and retrieving data from a database.

SELECT column1, column2, ...
FROM table_name;

SELECT: Specifies that you want to retrieve data.
column1, column2, ...: Names of the columns you want to retrieve. You can use * to select all columns.
FROM: Specifies the table from which you want to retrieve data.
table_name: Name of the table containing the data.
Example:

```
SELECT first_name, last_name
FROM employees;
```

Filtering Data with WHERE Clause:

The WHERE clause is used to filter rows based on specific conditions.

SELECT column1, column2, ...
FROM table_name
WHERE condition;

condition: The condition that rows must satisfy.
Example:

```
SELECT product_name, price
FROM products
WHERE price > 50;
```

Sorting Data with ORDER BY Clause:

The ORDER BY clause sorts the result set based on one or more columns.

SELECT column1, column2, ...
FROM table_name
ORDER BY column_to_sort [ASC|DESC];

SELECT column1, column2, ...
FROM table_name
ORDER BY column_to_sort [ASC|DESC];
Example:

```
SELECT employee_id, last_name, hire_date
FROM employees
ORDER BY hire_date DESC;
```

Inserting Data with INSERT INTO:

The INSERT INTO statement is used to add new records (rows) to a table.

INSERT INTO table_name (column1, column2, ...)
VALUES (value1, value2, ...);

Example:

```
INSERT INTO customers (customer_name, email, phone)
VALUES ('Ram', 'ram@example.com', '555-123-4567');
```

Updating Data with UPDATE:
UPDATE table_name
SET column1 = new_value1, column2 = new_value2, ...
WHERE condition;

Example:

```
UPDATE products
SET price = 25.99
WHERE product_id = 101;
```

Deleting Data with DELETE:
The DELETE statement removes records from a table.
DELETE FROM table_name
WHERE condition;
Example:

```
DELETE FROM customers
WHERE customer_id = 201;
```

These SQL basics are the foundation for working with Microsoft SQL Server databases. They enable you to perform various data manipulation tasks, from querying and retrieving data to inserting, updating, and deleting records. As you become more familiar with SQL, you can explore more advanced topics and queries to harness the full power of your database system.

2.2 SQL Data Types

In Microsoft SQL Server, data types define the kind of data that can be stored in a database column. SQL Server provides a variety of data types to accommodate different types of data, such as integers, text, dates, and more. Let's explore the SQL data types in SQL Server in detail:
Numeric Data Types:
These data types are used for storing numeric values, including integers and decimals.
Common numeric data types include:
INT: Represents a 32-bit signed integer.
BIGINT: Stores a 64-bit signed integer.
SMALLINT: Holds a 16-bit signed integer.
DECIMAL or NUMERIC: Used for fixed-point numbers with a specified precision and scale.
FLOAT: Stores approximate numeric values with a floating-point precision.
Character String Data Types:
These data types are used for storing character strings and textual data.
Common character string data types include:
CHAR(n): Fixed-length character string with a specified length n.
VARCHAR(n): Variable-length character string with a maximum length of n.
TEXT: Stores large blocks of text data, suitable for long documents.
Binary Data Types:
These data types are used for storing binary data, such as images or files.
Common binary data types include:
BINARY(n): Fixed-length binary data with a specified length n.
VARBINARY(n): Variable-length binary data with a maximum length of n.
IMAGE: Stores large binary data, such as images or multimedia files.
Date and Time Data Types:
These data types are used for storing date and time values.
Common date and time data types include:

DATE: Stores date values only.
TIME: Stores time values.
DATETIME or DATETIME2: Stores date and time values with fractional seconds precision.
SMALLDATETIME: Stores date and time values with reduced precision for storage efficiency.
Boolean Data Type:
SQL Server does not have a dedicated Boolean data type. Instead, it uses BIT, which can represent 0 (false), 1 (true), or NULL (unknown).
Uniqueidentifier Data Type:
UNIQUEIDENTIFIER stores a globally unique identifier (GUID). It is often used as a primary key for replication and distributed systems.
Other Specialized Data Types:
SQL Server provides several specialized data types for specific purposes, including:
XML: Stores XML data.
SQL_VARIANT: Stores values of different data types.
GEOMETRY and GEOGRAPHY: Used for spatial data, such as geographic coordinates.
HIERARCHYID: Stores hierarchical data.
TIMESTAMP (deprecated): Used for versioning and tracking changes.
User-Defined Data Types (UDTs):
SQL Server allows you to create custom data types based on existing data types. These user-defined data types can simplify database design and enforce data consistency.
Choosing the appropriate data type is essential for efficient storage and data integrity. It's important to consider factors like data size, precision, and the nature of the data when selecting a data type for a column in your database schema. Proper data type selection can help optimize database performance and ensure data accuracy.

2.3 Creating and Managing Databases

Creating and managing databases in Microsoft SQL Server is a fundamental aspect of database administration. Here, we'll explain the process of creating and managing databases in SQL Server:
Creating a Database:
To create a new database in SQL Server, you can use SQL Server Management Studio (SSMS) or write SQL statements. Here's how to create a database using SSMS:
Open SQL Server Management Studio.
Connect to your SQL Server instance.
In the Object Explorer, right-click on "Databases."
Select "New Database."
Provide a name for your database.
Configure the database settings, such as the file locations, initial size, and growth options.
Click "OK" to create the database.
If you prefer using SQL statements, you can use the CREATE DATABASE command:

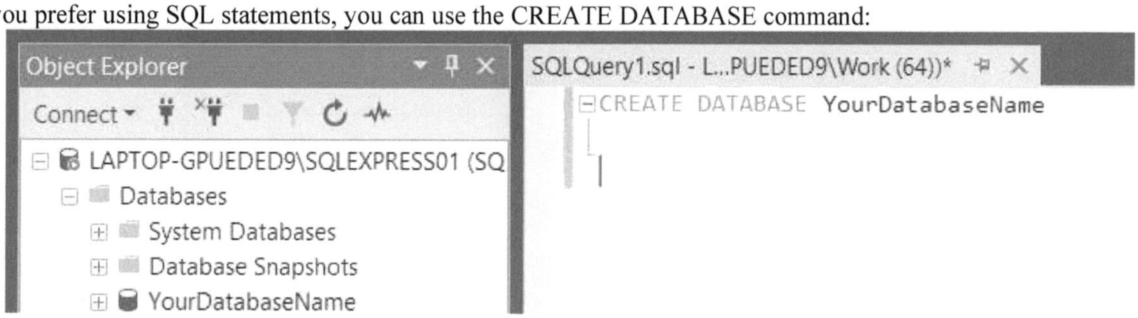

Managing Database Properties:
After creating a database, you can manage its properties to fine-tune its behavior. Some important properties include:
Filegroups: SQL Server allows you to organize database files into filegroups. You can create and manage filegroups to optimize data storage and backups.
Collation: Specify the collation for the database, which determines how string comparisons and sorting are performed.
Recovery Model: Choose the appropriate recovery model based on your backup and recovery requirements. Options include Full, Simple, and Bulk-Logged.

Compatibility Level: Set the compatibility level to control how the database behaves with regard to older SQL Server versions.

Creating Tables:

Once the database is created, you can create tables to store data. Use the CREATE TABLE statement to define the table's structure, including column names, data types, constraints, and indexes.

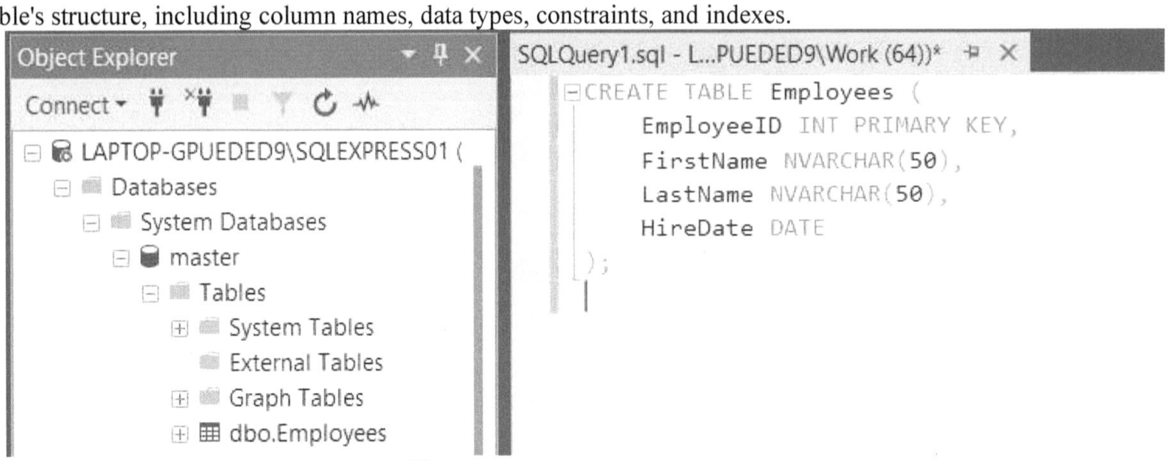

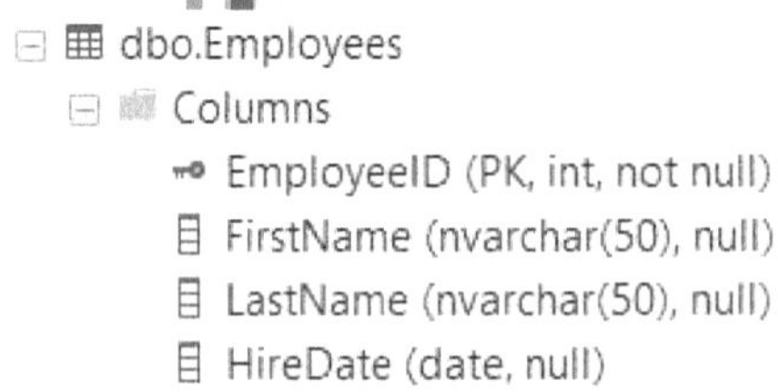

Managing Data:

You can insert, update, and delete data in your tables using SQL statements. For example:

INSERT INTO is used to add new rows of data.

UPDATE is used to modify existing data.

DELETE is used to remove data.

```
INSERT INTO Employees (EmployeeID, FirstName, LastName, HireDate)
VALUES (1, 'Ram', 'Sharma', '2022-01-15');
UPDATE Employees
SET FirstName = 'Sham'
WHERE EmployeeID = 1;

DELETE FROM Employees
WHERE EmployeeID = 1;
```

Output:

Indexing:

To optimize query performance, you can create indexes on columns that are frequently used in search and join operations. SQL Server provides different types of indexes, including clustered and non-clustered indexes.

Backup and Restore:

Regularly back up your databases to prevent data loss. SQL Server offers various backup and restore options. You can use SSMS or SQL statements like BACKUP DATABASE and RESTORE DATABASE to manage backups.

Security and Permissions:
SQL Server allows you to control access to your database by setting permissions and roles. You can create logins, users, and assign specific permissions to control who can view, modify, or administer the database.
Maintenance Plans:
SQL Server includes tools for creating maintenance plans to automate tasks like backups, index rebuilds, and database consistency checks.
Monitoring and Optimization:
Use SQL Server's built-in tools and performance monitoring features to identify and resolve performance issues. SQL Profiler, Query Store, and Dynamic Management Views (DMVs) are valuable resources for optimization.
Dropping Databases:
To remove a database, you can use the `DROP DATABASE` statement:
DROP DATABASE YourDatabaseName;

Be cautious when dropping databases, as this action permanently deletes all data and objects associated with the database.

2.4 Creating and Modifying Tables

In Microsoft SQL Server, creating and modifying tables involves defining the structure of your database by specifying columns, data types, constraints, and relationships. Here's a detailed guide with examples:
Creating Tables:

```
Syntax for Table Creation:
CREATE TABLE table_name (
   column1 datatype constraint,
   column2 datatype constraint,
   ...
);
```

Example:
Let's create a simple table called "Employees" with various columns:

```
CREATE TABLE Employees (
    EmployeeID INT PRIMARY KEY,
    FirstName NVARCHAR(50),
    LastName NVARCHAR(50),
    Email NVARCHAR(100) UNIQUE,
    DepartmentID INT,
    CONSTRAINT FK_Department FOREIGN KEY (DepartmentID) REFERENCES Departments(DepartmentID)
);
```

EmployeeID is the primary key for uniquely identifying each employee.
FirstName, **LastName**, and **Email** are columns for storing employee details.
DepartmentID is a foreign key referencing the Departments table.
Modifying Tables:
Adding a New Column:

```
ALTER TABLE table_name
ADD column_name datatype constraint;
```

Example:
Adding a new column "PhoneNumber" to the Employees table:

```
ALTER TABLE Employees
ADD PhoneNumber VARCHAR(15);
```

Modifying a Column:

```sql
ALTER TABLE table_name
ALTER COLUMN column_name new_datatype constraint;
```

Example:
Changing the data type of the PhoneNumber column:

```sql
ALTER TABLE Employees
ALTER COLUMN PhoneNumber INT;
```

Dropping a Column:

```sql
ALTER TABLE table_name
DROP COLUMN column_name;
```

Example:
Dropping the PhoneNumber column:

```sql
ALTER TABLE Employees
DROP COLUMN PhoneNumber;
```

Adding a Constraint:

```sql
ALTER TABLE table_name
ADD CONSTRAINT constraint_name constraint_type (columns);
```

Example:
Adding a check constraint to ensure employees are above a certain age:

```sql
ALTER TABLE Employees
ADD CONSTRAINT CHK_Age CHECK (Age >= 18);
```

Conclusion:
Creating and modifying tables in Microsoft SQL Server involves using SQL statements like **CREATE TABLE** and **ALTER TABLE** to define the structure and properties of your database. These commands allow you to add, modify, or remove columns, constraints, and relationships as needed, ensuring your database schema remains aligned with evolving business requirements.

2.5 SQL Server Management Studio (SSMS)

SQL Server Management Studio (SSMS) is a powerful integrated environment for managing, configuring, and administering Microsoft SQL Server databases. It provides a wide range of tools and features that make it easier to work with SQL Server instances and databases. Here's an overview of SQL Server Management Studio:

Query Editor:
The Query Editor in SSMS allows you to write and execute SQL queries, scripts, and stored procedures. It provides syntax highlighting, code completion, and debugging features to facilitate query development.

Object Explorer:
Object Explorer is a tree-like view that displays the hierarchy of SQL Server instances, databases, tables, views, stored procedures, and other objects. You can use it to navigate, manage, and interact with database objects.

Database Management:
SSMS enables you to create, modify, and delete databases. You can also manage database properties, configure security settings, and perform backup and restore operations.

Server Management:
You can use SSMS to manage SQL Server instances, including configuring server properties, setting up server security, and monitoring server performance.

Import and Export Data:
SSMS provides wizards for importing and exporting data to and from SQL Server databases. This feature is helpful for transferring data between different database systems.

Query Performance Tuning:
SSMS includes tools for analysing query performance, generating execution plans, and identifying bottlenecks. This helps optimize database queries and improve overall system performance.

Reporting and Visualization:

You can create and design reports using SQL Server Reporting Services (SSRS) directly within SSMS. SSRS allows you to generate, schedule, and distribute reports to users.

Integration with Source Control:

SSMS can integrate with version control systems like Git, making it easier to manage database changes and collaborate with development teams.

Templates and Snippets:

SSMS offers code templates and snippets to expedite the creation of SQL scripts. This feature is useful for writing repetitive code segments.

Security Management:

SSMS allows you to configure security settings, manage user accounts, and set permissions for database objects. You can also audit and monitor security-related events.

Extended Features:

SSMS supports various extensions and add-ons that extend its functionality, such as third-party plugins and custom scripts.

Compatibility:

SSMS is compatible with multiple versions of Microsoft SQL Server, making it a versatile tool for database administrators and developers.

SQL Server Management Studio is an essential tool for anyone working with Microsoft SQL Server databases. It streamlines database administration tasks, enhances query development, and provides a comprehensive environment for managing SQL Server instances and data effectively.

2.6 Exercise

Exercise 1 – MCQ

1. Which keyword is used to retrieve data from a SQL database?
a) GET
b) SELECT
c) RETRIEVE
d) FETCH
2. What does SQL stand for?
a) Simple Query Language
b) Structured Query Language
c) Systematic Question Logic
d) Structured Question Language
3. Which data type is used to store a date and time in SQL?
a) VARCHAR
b) INT
c) DATETIME
d) BOOLEAN
4. Which data type is appropriate for storing large text values in SQL Server?
a) TEXT
b) CHAR
c) VARCHAR(MAX)
d) NVARCHAR
5. Which SQL statement is used to create a new database?
a) CREATE DATABASE
b) NEW DATABASE
c) ADD DATABASE
d) INITIATE DATABASE
6. Which command is used to delete a database in SQL?
a) REMOVE DATABASE
b) DELETE DATABASE
c) DROP DATABASE
d) ERASE DATABASE

7. What is the command to add a new column to an existing table in SQL?
a) INSERT COLUMN
b) ADD COLUMN
c) ALTER COLUMN
d) CREATE COLUMN
8. Which constraint is used to ensure that each row in a column has a unique value?
a) UNIQUE
b) PRIMARY KEY
c) INDEX
d) FOREIGN KEY
9. Which feature of SSMS allows users to visually design database schemas?
a) Object Explorer
b) Query Editor
c) Table Designer
d) Activity Monitor
10. Which tool in SSMS allows users to view and manage database security, including user permissions?
a) Database Engine Tuning Advisor
b) Security Manager
c) SQL Server Profiler
d) SQL Server Management Studio doesn't provide this feature

Exercise 2 – True/False

1. SQL stands for Structured Query Language and is used to manage and manipulate relational databases.
2. In SQL, the VARCHAR data type is used for storing variable-length character strings.
3. A single SQL Server instance can contain multiple databases, allowing for logical separation of data.
4. The ALTER TABLE statement in SQL is used to add or delete columns from an existing table.
5. SQL Server Management Studio (SSMS) is a graphical user interface (GUI) used to interact with SQL Server databases.
6. SQL commands such as SELECT, INSERT, UPDATE, and DELETE are used to perform CRUD (Create, Read, Update, Delete) operations on data.
7. The DECIMAL data type in SQL is used for storing exact numeric values with a fixed precision and scale.
8. The DROP DATABASE statement in SQL is used to permanently delete a database and its contents.
9. PRIMARY KEY constraints ensure that each row in a table is unique and cannot contain NULL values.
10. SSMS provides tools for database administrators to perform tasks like backup, restore, and security management for SQL Server databases.

Exercise 3 – Fill in the blanks

1. "SELECT * FROM __________" is a basic SQL query used to retrieve all columns and rows from a table.
2. In SQL, the __________ data type is commonly used to store a fixed-length string.
3. The SQL command used to create a new database is "CREATE __________ database_name".
4. The SQL command to add a new column to an existing table is "ALTER TABLE table_name __________ column_name data_type".
5. SSMS provides a graphical user interface for __________ with SQL Server databases.
6. The clause used to filter records in a SQL query is "__________ BY" followed by conditions.
7. The SQL data type "__________" is used to store date and time values.
8. The command "DROP __________ database_name" is used to delete a database.
9. A primary key is a column or a set of columns that uniquely identifies each __________ in a table.
10. SSMS allows users to write and execute __________ queries against SQL Server databases.

Exercise 4 – One word answer

1. What does SQL stand for?

2. Name a numeric SQL data type.
3. What command is used to create a database in SQL?
4. Which SQL clause creates a new table?
5. What is the full form of SSMS?
6. Define 'Query'.
7. Mention a date/time SQL data type.
8. How do you drop a database in SQL?
9. What SQL command alters a table's structure?
10. What does SSMS provide for SQL Server administration?

Exercise 5 – Small answer

1. Define SQL and its primary purpose in databases.
2. What are the components of a basic SQL query?
3. Explain the importance of data types in SQL.
4. Differentiate between CHAR and VARCHAR data types in SQL.
5. What is the SQL command used to create a new database?
6. Explain the purpose of the 'USE' statement in SQL.
7. What is a primary key, and why is it important when creating tables?
8. How do you add a new column to an existing table in SQL?
9. What functionalities does SQL Server Management Studio (SSMS) offer for database administrators?
10. How can SSMS assist in optimizing SQL queries?

Exercise 6 – Long answer

1. Explain the fundamental structure of a SQL query and its components. Provide an example query demonstrating SELECT, FROM, WHERE, GROUP BY, and ORDER BY clauses.
2. Detail the significance of data types in SQL. Elaborate on at least five commonly used data types, their attributes, and scenarios where they are best applied.
3. Describe the step-by-step process of creating a new database in SQL Server, emphasizing considerations like naming conventions, filegroups, and growth options.
4. Explain the process of creating a table in SQL Server, covering primary keys, foreign keys, constraints, and their roles in defining table structures. Provide an example table creation script.
5. Detail the primary features and functionalities of SQL Server Management Studio (SSMS). Discuss how it aids in database administration, query execution, and overall management of SQL Server instances.
6. Discuss the concept of normalization in table design. Explain the different normal forms and their importance in maintaining a well-structured database.
7. Explain the role of DML statements (INSERT, UPDATE, DELETE) in SQL. Provide examples for each statement and describe their impact on data integrity.
8. Elaborate on the importance of constraints and indexes in SQL tables. Discuss various types of constraints and indexes and their significance in database performance and data integrity.
9. Define the ACID properties and explain how transactions ensure data integrity. Provide a detailed example of a transaction and its impact on maintaining consistency in a database.
10. Differentiate between stored procedures and functions in SQL Server. Explain their respective use cases, advantages, and limitations, and provide examples illustrating their implementation.

Answer

Exercise 1:
Answer: 1: b, 2: b, 3: c, 4: c, 5: a, 6: c, 7: b, 8: a, 9: c, 10: b
Exercise 2:
Answer: 1: True, 2: True, 3: True, 4: True, 5: True, 6: True 7: True, 8: True, 9: True, 10: True
Exercise 3:
Answer: 1: table_name,2: CHAR, 3: DATABASE, 4: ADD, 5: INTERACTING, 6: WHERE, 7: DATETIME, 8: DATABASE, 9: RECORD/ROW, 10: SQL

ONLINE RESOURCES

Practice Paper
Link: https://forms.office.com/r/NeCURkErcA?origin=lprLink
QR Code:

Chapter 3: SQL Queries and Data Manipulation

3.1 SELECT Statements

In Microsoft SQL, the SELECT statement is a fundamental SQL command used to retrieve data from one or more tables. It allows you to specify the columns you want to retrieve, apply filters, sort the results, and more. Here's an overview of the SELECT statement in Microsoft SQL:

Basic SELECT Syntax:

```
SELECT column1, column2, ...
FROM table_name;
```

Retrieving All Columns:

```
SELECT *
FROM employees;
```

Filtering Rows with WHERE Clause:

```
SELECT column1, column2, ...
FROM table_name
WHERE condition;
```

Example:

```
SELECT product_name, price
FROM products
WHERE price > 50;
```

Sorting Results with ORDER BY Clause:

```
SELECT column1, column2, ...
FROM table_name
ORDER BY column_to_sort [ASC|DESC];
```

Using Aliases:

```
SELECT first_name AS "First Name", last_name AS "Last Name"
FROM employees;
```

Removing Duplicate Rows with DISTINCT:

```
SELECT DISTINCT department_id
FROM employees;
```

Combining Columns:

```
SELECT first_name || ' ' || last_name AS "Full Name"
FROM employees;
```

Combining Filtering and Sorting:

You can use both the WHERE and ORDER BY clauses in a single query to retrieve and order data based on specific criteria.

```
SELECT column1, column2, ...
FROM table_name
WHERE condition
ORDER BY column_to_sort [ASC|DESC];
```

Limiting Rows with LIMIT (MySQL-specific):

```
SELECT first_name, last_name
FROM employees
LIMIT 5;
```

Aggregate Functions:

MySQL supports various aggregate functions like SUM, AVG, COUNT, MIN, and MAX for summarizing and calculating data.

```
SELECT department_id, AVG(salary) AS "Average Salary"
FROM employees
GROUP BY department_id;
```

The SELECT statement in Microsoft SQL is a versatile tool for retrieving and manipulating data. By combining various clauses, functions, and operators, you can tailor your queries to meet specific data retrieval and analysis requirements. Understanding these SQL concepts is essential for working effectively with Microsoft SQL databases.

3.2 Filtering and Sorting Data

Filtering and sorting data are fundamental operations when working with databases, and Microsoft SQL provides powerful capabilities to perform these tasks. Here's an overview of how to filter and sort data in Microsoft SQL:

Filtering Data with the `WHERE` Clause:

The `WHERE` clause is used to filter rows based on specified conditions.

```
SELECT column1, column2, ...
FROM table_name
WHERE condition;
```

- column1, column2, ...: Columns to retrieve.
- table_name: Name of the table.
- condition: The condition that rows must satisfy.

Example:

```
SELECT product_name, price
FROM products
WHERE price > 50;
```

Sorting Data with the `ORDER BY` Clause:

The `ORDER BY` clause is used to sort the result set based on one or more columns.

```
SELECT column1, column2, ...
FROM table_name
ORDER BY column_to_sort [ASC|DESC];
```

- column_to_sort: The column by which to sort the result.
- ASC: Ascending order (default).
- DESC: Descending order.

Example:

```
SELECT employee_id, last_name, hire_date
FROM employees
ORDER BY hire_date DESC;
```

Combining Filtering and Sorting:

You can use both the `WHERE` and `ORDER BY` clauses in a single query to retrieve and order data based on specific criteria.

```
SELECT column1, column2, ...
FROM table_name
WHERE condition
ORDER BY column_to_sort [ASC|DESC];
```

Example:

```
SELECT first_name, last_name, hire_date
FROM employees
WHERE department_id = 30
ORDER BY hire_date;
```

Removing Duplicate Rows with `DISTINCT`:
The `DISTINCT` keyword ensures that only unique values are retrieved.

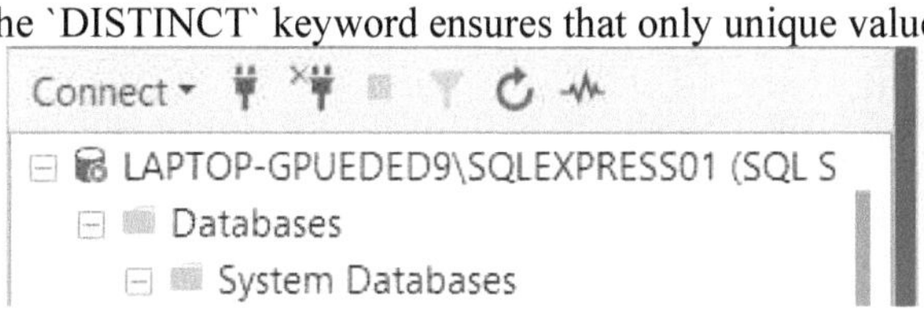


```
SELECT DISTINCT department_id
FROM employees;
```

3.3 Joins and Subqueries

Joins and subqueries are advanced SQL techniques that allow you to retrieve and manipulate data from multiple tables and apply complex conditions. Microsoft SQL provides robust support for both joins and subqueries. Here's a detailed overview of how to use joins and subqueries effectively in Microsoft SQL:

Joins:
Joins are used to combine rows from two or more tables based on related columns. There are various types of joins in MySQL:

INNER JOIN: An inner join returns only the rows that have matching values in both tables.

```
SELECT customers.customer_name, orders.order_date
FROM customers
INNER JOIN orders ON customers.customer_id = orders.customer_id;
```

LEFT JOIN (or LEFT OUTER JOIN):
A left join returns all rows from the left table and the matched rows from the right table. If there is no match, NULL values are returned for the right table.

```
SELECT employees.first_name, departments.department_name
FROM employees
LEFT JOIN departments ON employees.department_id = departments.department_id;
```

RIGHT JOIN (or RIGHT OUTER JOIN):
A right join returns all rows from the right table and the matched rows from the left table. If there is no match, NULL values are returned for the left table.

```
SELECT products.product_name, order_details.quantity
FROM products
RIGHT JOIN order_details ON products.product_id = order_details.product_id;
```

FULL OUTER JOIN:
A full outer join returns all rows from both tables. If there is no match, NULL values are returned for the columns from the non-matching table.

```
SELECT customers.customer_name, orders.order_id
FROM customers
FULL OUTER JOIN orders ON customers.customer_id = orders.customer_id;
```

Subqueries:
Subqueries, also known as nested queries or inner queries, are queries embedded within another SQL statement. They can be used in various parts of a SQL statement, such as the SELECT, FROM, WHERE, and HAVING clauses.

Scalar Subquery:
A scalar subquery returns a single value and can be used in any place where a single value is expected.

```
SELECT product_name, price
FROM products
WHERE price > (SELECT AVG(price) FROM products);
```

Correlated Subquery:
A correlated subquery refers to columns from the outer query and is evaluated once for each row processed by the outer query.

```
SELECT employee_name, salary
FROM employees e
WHERE salary > (SELECT AVG(salary) FROM employees WHERE department_id = e.department_id);
```

Subquery in the FROM Clause (Derived Table):
You can use a subquery in the FROM clause to create a derived table, which can be treated like a regular table in the outer query.

```
SELECT department_name, AVG(salary) AS avg_salary
FROM (SELECT * FROM employees WHERE salary > 50000) filtered_employees
GROUP BY department_name;
```

Subquery in the WHERE Clause:
Subqueries in the WHERE clause are often used to filter rows based on values from another table.

```
SELECT customer_name
FROM customers
WHERE customer_id IN (
SELECT customer_id
FROM orders
WHERE order_date >= TO_DATE('2022-02-01', 'YYYY-MM-DD')
);
```

Joins and subqueries are powerful tools in MySQL for querying and retrieving data from complex database structures. They allow you to extract meaningful information from related tables, apply conditional logic, and perform advanced data manipulation. Understanding when and how to use joins and subqueries is crucial for effective SQL query writing.

3.4 Inserting, Updating, and Deleting Data

In Microsoft SQL, you can perform various operations to manipulate data in tables, including inserting new records, updating existing records, and deleting records. These operations are crucial for maintaining the integrity and accuracy of your database. Here's how to perform these tasks:

Inserting Data:
The INSERT statement is used to add new records (rows) to a table. There are two primary ways to insert data into a table:

Inserting Data into Specific Columns:

```
INSERT INTO table_name (column1, column2, ...)
VALUES (value1, value2, ...);
```

table_name: Name of the table.
column1, column2, ...: Names of the columns you want to insert data into.
value1, value2, ...: Values you want to insert into the specified columns.

Examples:

```
INSERT INTO customers (customer_name, email, phone)
VALUES ('John Smith', 'john@example.com', '555-123-4567');
```

Inserting Data into All Columns:
If you want to insert data into all columns of a table, you can omit the column list.

```
INSERT INTO table_name
VALUES (value1, value2, ...);
```

Examples:

```
INSERT INTO employees
VALUES (101, 'Alice', 'Johnson', '2020-03-15', 'HR', 45000);
```

Updating Data:
The UPDATE statement is used to modify existing records in a table.

UPDATE table_name
SET column1 = new_value1, column2 = new_value2, ...
WHERE condition;

table_name: Name of the table.
column1, column2, ...: Columns you want to update.
new_value1, new_value2, ...: New values you want to set for the specified columns.
condition: Condition that determines which rows to update.

Examples:

```
UPDATE products
SET price = 25.99
WHERE product_id = 101
```

Deleting Data:
The DELETE statement is used to remove records from a table.

DELETE FROM table_name
WHERE condition;

table_name: Name of the table.
condition: Condition that specifies which rows to delete.

Example:

```
DELETE FROM customers
WHERE customer_id = 201;
```

Note: Be cautious when using the DELETE statement, as it permanently removes data from the table.
Batch Operations:
You can perform batch operations to insert, update, or delete multiple records at once by using appropriate conditions or specifying multiple sets of values in the INSERT statement.
These data manipulation operations are essential for maintaining data consistency and making changes to your Microsoft SQL database. Always ensure that you have proper backups and thoroughly test your SQL statements before performing data manipulation operations, especially updates and deletes, to avoid unintended data loss or corruption.

3.5 Exercise

Exercise 1 – MCQ

1. Which keyword is used to retrieve specific columns from a table in SQL?
A) FETCH
B) SHOW
C) SELECT
D) VIEW
2. To filter data in SQL, which clause is used?
A) WHERE
B) LIMIT
C) GROUP BY
D) HAVING
3. Which type of join retrieves records that have matching values in both tables?
A) RIGHT JOIN
B) OUTER JOIN

C) INNER JOIN
D) LEFT JOIN
4. In SQL, what function is used to add new rows of data into a table?
A) INSERT INTO
B) ADD ROW
C) CREATE ROW
D) APPEND ROW
5. Which SQL statement is used to modify existing records in a table?
A) ALTER
B) UPDATE
C) CHANGE
D) SET
6. What is the purpose of the ORDER BY clause in SQL?
A) To filter data based on conditions
B) To sort data in ascending or descending order
C) To join tables from different databases
D) To insert new rows into a table
7. Which join returns all records from the left table and the matched records from the right table?
A) INNER JOIN
B) LEFT JOIN
C) OUTER JOIN
D) CROSS JOIN
8. What keyword is used to delete records from a table in SQL?
A) ERASE
B) DROP
C) DELETE
D) REMOVE
9. Which clause is used to specify a condition for grouping rows when using aggregate functions?
A) GROUP BY
B) ARRANGE BY
C) CLASSIFY BY
D) SORT BY
10. What is the purpose of a subquery in SQL?
A) To retrieve data from multiple tables
B) To define the structure of a new table
C) To perform calculations on columns
D) To nest within another SQL statement for more complex queries

Exercise 2 – True/ False

1. The SELECT statement in SQL can be used to retrieve data from multiple tables simultaneously.
2. The WHERE clause in SQL is used to sort the retrieved data in ascending or descending order
3. Joins in SQL are exclusively used to combine data from tables having a one-to-one relationship.
4. The DELETE statement in SQL removes only the table structure, leaving the data intact.
5. The SELECT statement cannot perform calculations or apply functions on retrieved data.
6. The HAVING clause in SQL works similarly to the WHERE clause but is specifically used with aggregate functions.
7. Subqueries in SQL are always executed before the outer query.
8. The INSERT statement in SQL allows the addition of multiple rows into a table in a single query.
9. The DISTINCT keyword in SQL is used to eliminate duplicate rows from the result set.
10. Inner joins in SQL return all rows from both tables being joined.

Exercise 3 – Fill in the blank

1. The ___ statement in SQL retrieves data from one or more tables based on specified criteria.
2. The ___ clause in SQL is used to filter records based on specified conditions.
3. ___ is used to arrange data in ascending or descending order in SQL.
4. ___ is a SQL operation that combines rows from two or more tables based on a related column between them.
5. A ___ is a query nested within another SQL query.
6. The ___ statement in SQL is used to add new records to a table.
7. The ___ statement in SQL is used to modify existing records in a table.
8. ___ is a SQL operation used to remove rows from a table.
9. The ___ clause in SQL is used to specify conditions while performing insert, update, or delete operations.
10. The ___ keyword is used to retrieve all columns from a table in SQL.

Exercise 4 – Match case

1) SELECT Statements
2) Filtering and Sorting Data
3) Joins and Subqueries
4) Inserting, Updating, and Deleting Data

a. Retrieves data from one or more tables.
b. Modifies existing records in a table.
c. Combines rows from two or more tables.
d. Narrows down rows based on specific conditions.

Exercise 5 – One word answer

1. What clause specifies the columns to retrieve in a SELECT statement?
2. Which keyword is used to filter data in a WHERE clause based on multiple conditions?
3. Which clause is used to combine rows from different tables based on a related column?
4. Which SQL command is used to add new records to a table?
5. Which keyword is used to modify existing records in a table?
6. Which SQL command removes rows from a table based on specified conditions?
7. Which clause is used to retrieve unique values in a specified column?
8. Which clause is used to sort the result set in ascending or descending order?
9. Which type of join returns records that have matching values in both tables?
10. What term refers to a query nested inside another query?

Exercise 6 – Small answer

1. Explain the purpose of the SELECT statement in SQL. Provide an example demonstrating the usage of aliases in SELECT statements.
2. How does the WHERE clause contribute to filtering data in SQL queries? Give an example showcasing the use of logical operators (AND, OR) in a WHERE clause.
3. Define a SQL join. Differentiate between INNER JOIN and OUTER JOIN. Provide an example demonstrating an INNER JOIN between two tables.
4. Describe the syntax for inserting data into a table in SQL. Provide an example of an INSERT statement inserting values into specific columns of a table.
5. Explain the UPDATE statement in SQL. Illustrate its use with an example updating multiple records based on a specified condition.
6. What is the purpose of the DELETE statement in SQL? Provide an example of using the DELETE statement with a WHERE clause.
7. How is data sorted in SQL? Explain the ORDER BY clause and its role in sorting query results. Provide an example sorting data in descending order.
8. Define a subquery in SQL. Explain the concept of a correlated subquery and how it differs from a regular subquery. Offer an example of a subquery.

9. Explain the difference between a UNION and a JOIN operation in SQL. When would you use one over the other? Provide an example of each

10. Discuss the usage of the CASE statement in SQL. Provide an example of using CASE to perform conditional operations in a SELECT query.

Exercise 7 – Long answer

1. Describe the anatomy of a SELECT statement in SQL, detailing each clause's role (SELECT, FROM, WHERE, GROUP BY, HAVING, ORDER BY). Provide an example demonstrating a complex SELECT query.
2. Explain the significance of the WHERE clause in SQL queries. Illustrate various conditional operators and functions used for filtering data with multiple examples.
3. Elaborate on aggregate functions in SQL (e.g., SUM, COUNT, AVG) and their application with the GROUP BY clause. Provide scenarios where these functions are useful and examples demonstrating their usage.
4. Discuss the ORDER BY clause in SQL queries. Explain its functionality, including sorting results in ascending and descending order, and how it can be combined with other clauses for effective data retrieval.
5. Describe the various types of SQL joins (e.g., INNER JOIN, LEFT JOIN, RIGHT JOIN, FULL JOIN). Explain their differences using examples and discuss scenarios where each type is best suited.
6. Explain the concept of subqueries in SQL. Provide examples demonstrating their usage in WHERE clauses, SELECT statements, and other scenarios where subqueries can be applied.
7. Detail the process of inserting data into SQL tables. Discuss different methods of data insertion (single-row, multi-row) and potential challenges that may arise during insertion.
8. Describe how the UPDATE statement modifies existing data in SQL tables. Include examples showcasing the UPDATE syntax and the impact of WHERE clauses on updating specific records.
9. Explain the DELETE statement's functionality and its implications on data removal from SQL tables. Discuss precautions and potential risks associated with deleting data, supported by examples.
10. Provide an in-depth explanation of combining multiple SQL operations (e.g., SELECT, INSERT, UPDATE, DELETE) within a single query. Illustrate scenarios where these combined operations prove beneficial.

Answer

Exercise 1:

Answer: 1: C, 2: A, 3: C, 4: A, 5: B, 6: B, 7: B, 8: C, 9: C, 10: D

Exercise 2:

Answer: 1: True, 2: False, 3: False, 4: False, 5: False, 6: False, 7: False, 8: True, 9: True, 10: False

Exercise 3:

Answer: 1: SELECT, 2: WHERE, 3: ORDER BY, 4: JOIN, 5: subquery, 6: INSERT, 7: UPDATE, 8: DELETE, 9: WHERE, 10: SELECT

Exercise 4

Answer 1: 1-a, 2-d, 3-c, 4-b.

ONLINE RESOURCES

Practice Paper

Link: https://forms.office.com/r/04F6JCrP5R?origin=lprLink

QR Code:

Chapter 4: Database Design and Normalization

4.1 Data Modelling

Data modeling in Microsoft SQL Server involves designing the structure of a database system. It focuses on defining tables, their relationships, constraints, and keys to efficiently store and manage data. Here's an overview of data modeling concepts in SQL Server:

Entity-Relationship (ER) Diagrams:

ER diagrams help visualize and define entities, attributes, and relationships between tables.

Normalization:

First Normal Form (1NF): Ensures atomicity by eliminating repeating groups within a table.

Second Normal Form (2NF): Makes sure no partial dependencies exist by separating subsets of data that apply to multiple rows.

Third Normal Form (3NF): Removes transitive dependencies by eliminating fields not dependent on the primary key.

Tables and Relationships:

Primary Keys: Unique identifiers for each record in a table.

Foreign Keys: Establish relationships between tables, maintaining referential integrity.

One-to-One, One-to-Many, and Many-to-Many Relationships: Define how entities relate to each other.

Data Types:

Integers, Strings, Dates, Decimals: Used to define columns in tables based on the nature of the data.

Example of Data Modeling in SQL Server:

Consider a library database:

Entities:

Books

BookID (Primary Key)

Title

AuthorID (Foreign Key)

Authors

AuthorID (Primary Key)

AuthorName

Genres

GenreID (Primary Key)

GenreName

Relationships:

Books - Authors: One-to-Many relationship (one author can write many books).

Books - Genres: Many-to-Many relationship (a book can belong to multiple genres, and a genre can have many books).

```sql
CREATE TABLE Authors (
    AuthorID INT PRIMARY KEY,
    AuthorName VARCHAR(100)
);

CREATE TABLE Books (
    BookID INT PRIMARY KEY,
    Title VARCHAR(255),
    AuthorID INT,
    GenreID INT,
    FOREIGN KEY (AuthorID) REFERENCES Authors(AuthorID),
    FOREIGN KEY (GenreID) REFERENCES Genres(GenreID)
);

CREATE TABLE Genres (
    GenreID INT PRIMARY KEY,
    GenreName VARCHAR(50)
);

CREATE TABLE BooksGenres (
    BookID INT,
    GenreID INT,
    PRIMARY KEY (BookID, GenreID),
    FOREIGN KEY (BookID) REFERENCES Books(BookID),
    FOREIGN KEY (GenreID) REFERENCES Genres(GenreID)
);
```

Queries:

Retrieving Books by Author:

SELECT Books.Title, Authors.AuthorName
FROM Books
JOIN Authors ON Books.AuthorID = Authors.AuthorID
WHERE Authors.AuthorName = 'J.K. Rowling';

This example demonstrates the basic setup of tables and relationships in a library database in SQL Server. Adjustments and additional tables may be required based on specific requirements and the complexity of the system.

4.2 Entity-Relationship Diagrams (ERD)

Entity-Relationship Diagrams (ERDs) in Microsoft SQL Server represent the logical structure of a database, illustrating entities, their attributes, and the relationships between entities. SQL Server Management Studio (SSMS) provides tools to create and visualize ERDs.

Components of an ERD:

Entities: Represent real-world objects stored in the database.

Attributes: Characteristics or properties of entities.

Relationships: Associations between entities.

Steps to Create an ERD in SQL Server Management Studio:

Open SSMS:

Open SQL Server Management Studio.

Connect to your SQL Server instance.

Create a Database Diagram:

Right-click on "Database Diagrams" within your target database.

Choose "New Database Diagram."

Add Tables:

Drag and drop tables from the "Tables" node onto the diagram.

This action automatically generates entities from the tables.

Define Relationships:

Create relationships between entities by dragging a primary key column to a foreign key column.

Double-click the relationship line to define properties, such as cardinality (one-to-one, one-to-many, many-to-many).

Example:

Consider a simple HR database:

Entities:

Employees

EmployeeID (Primary Key)
FirstName
LastName
DepartmentID (Foreign Key)

Departments

DepartmentID (Primary Key)
DepartmentName

Relationships:

Employees to Departments: One-to-Many (one department can have many employees).

Here's how you might represent this in an ERD using SQL Server Management Studio:

Creating Tables:

```
CREATE TABLE Departments (
    DepartmentID INT PRIMARY KEY,
    DepartmentName VARCHAR(50)
);

CREATE TABLE Employees (
    EmployeeID INT PRIMARY KEY,
    FirstName VARCHAR(50),
    LastName VARCHAR(50),
    DepartmentID INT FOREIGN KEY REFERENCES Departments(DepartmentID)
);
```

ERD Visualization in SSMS:

After creating the tables, open SSMS.

Navigate to your database, right-click "Database Diagrams," and select "New Database Diagram."

Drag the "Employees" and "Departments" tables onto the diagram.

Define the relationship between the "DepartmentID" columns.

The resulting ERD should show two entities (Employees and Departments) connected by a relationship line indicating the association between them.

Note:

ERDs provide a visual representation of database structure but don't display the complete schema.

You can add more details, such as additional attributes and relationships, to design a comprehensive ERD that captures the database's structure and connections.

4.3 Normalization Concepts

Normalization in Microsoft SQL Server is the process of organizing data in a database to eliminate redundancy and dependency, ensuring data integrity and efficiency. It follows a set of rules to structure databases into multiple related tables, reducing redundancy and anomalies.

Normal Forms in SQL Server:

First Normal Form (1NF):

Atomic Values: Each column should contain only atomic (indivisible) values.

Example:

```
CREATE TABLE Employees (
    EmployeeID INT PRIMARY KEY,
    FullName VARCHAR(100),
    PhoneNumbers VARCHAR(50)
);
```

To normalize to 1NF, separate phone numbers into a separate table:

```sql
CREATE TABLE Employees (
    EmployeeID INT PRIMARY KEY,
    FullName VARCHAR(100)
);

CREATE TABLE EmployeePhoneNumbers (
    EmployeeID INT,
    PhoneNumber VARCHAR(15),
    PRIMARY KEY (EmployeeID, PhoneNumber),
    FOREIGN KEY (EmployeeID) REFERENCES Employees(EmployeeID)
);
```

Second Normal Form (2NF):

1NF + No Partial Dependencies: All non-key columns should depend on the entire primary key.

Example:

```sql
CREATE TABLE OrderDetails (
    OrderID INT,
    ProductID INT,
    ProductName VARCHAR(100),
    Quantity INT,
    PRIMARY KEY (OrderID, ProductID)
);
```

To normalize to 2NF, separate product details into a separate table:

```sql
CREATE TABLE Products (
    ProductID INT PRIMARY KEY,
    ProductName VARCHAR(100)
);

CREATE TABLE OrderProducts (
    OrderID INT,
    ProductID INT,
    Quantity INT,
    PRIMARY KEY (OrderID, ProductID),
    FOREIGN KEY (ProductID) REFERENCES Products(ProductID)
);
```

Third Normal Form (3NF):

2NF + No Transitive Dependencies: Eliminate columns not directly dependent on the primary key.

Example:

```sql
CREATE TABLE Employees (
    EmployeeID INT PRIMARY KEY,
    FullName VARCHAR(100),
    DepartmentID INT,
    DepartmentName VARCHAR(50)
);
```

To normalize to 3NF, create a separate Departments table:

```sql
CREATE TABLE Employees (
    EmployeeID INT PRIMARY KEY,
    FullName VARCHAR(100),
    DepartmentID INT,
    FOREIGN KEY (DepartmentID) REFERENCES Departments(DepartmentID)
);

CREATE TABLE Departments (
    DepartmentID INT PRIMARY KEY,
    DepartmentName VARCHAR(50)
);
```

Benefits of Normalization:
Reduces redundancy, saving storage space.
Prevents data anomalies like insertion, update, and deletion anomalies.
Enhances data consistency and integrity.
Considerations:
Over-normalization can lead to increased complexity in queries requiring JOIN operations.
Finding the right balance between normalization and performance is crucial based on specific application needs.

4.4 Design Best Practices

Designing a database in Microsoft SQL Server involves adhering to best practices to ensure optimal performance, scalability, and maintainability. Here are key design principles and practices:
Normalization:
Normalize the database to eliminate redundancy and ensure data integrity by minimizing data duplication. This includes breaking down large tables into smaller, related tables.
Use of Primary Keys and Indexing:
Primary Keys: Assign a primary key to each table for uniqueness and to establish relationships.
Indexes: Implement appropriate indexes on columns frequently used in queries to enhance search performance. Be cautious not to over-index, as it can impact write operations.
Data Types and Constraints:
Choose suitable data types for columns to optimize storage and retrieval. Use constraints (NOT NULL, UNIQUE, CHECK) to enforce data integrity and validity.
Relationships and Foreign Keys:
Define relationships between tables using foreign keys to maintain referential integrity.
Use cascade options cautiously to manage the deletion or update of related records.
Stored Procedures and Views:
Stored Procedures: Utilize stored procedures for frequently executed queries to improve performance and security.
Views: Abstract complex queries into views to simplify data access and enhance security.
Partitioning and Filegroups:
Implement table and index partitioning to improve manageability, query performance, and maintenance tasks.
Distribute data across filegroups to manage storage more efficiently.
Backup and Recovery Strategy:
Establish a robust backup plan to protect against data loss and ensure quick recovery in case of failures. Regularly test backups to verify their integrity.
Example of Best Practices:
Employee Database Schema:
Consider an employee database:

```sql
CREATE TABLE Employees (
    EmployeeID INT PRIMARY KEY,
    FirstName VARCHAR(50),
    LastName VARCHAR(50),
    Email VARCHAR(100) UNIQUE,
    DepartmentID INT,
    CONSTRAINT FK_Department FOREIGN KEY (DepartmentID) REFERENCES Departments(DepartmentID)
);

CREATE TABLE Departments (
    DepartmentID INT PRIMARY KEY,
    DepartmentName VARCHAR(50)
);
```

This simple schema follows best practices by:
Defining primary and foreign keys for relationships.
Using appropriate data types and constraints (e.g., UNIQUE constraint on email).
Normalizing data by separating employees and departments into distinct tables.
Indexing:
Adding an index on the DepartmentID column in the Employees table for faster queries:

```sql
CREATE INDEX IX_DepartmentID ON Employees(DepartmentID);
```

This index speeds up searches when querying based on department information.

Conclusion:

Adhering to these best practices helps in creating a robust, scalable, and well-performing SQL Server database. Always consider specific application requirements and data usage patterns to fine-tune the design for optimal performance.

4.5 Exercise

Exercise 1 – MCQ

1. Which of the following is not a key concept in data modeling?
A) Entities
B) Relationships
C) Indexing
D) Attributes
2. In an ER diagram, a diamond shape represents:
A) Entity
B) Attribute
C) Relationship
D) Key
3. What is the primary goal of normalization in database design?
A) Minimize storage space
B) Reduce redundancy and anomalies
C) Maximize query performance
D) Optimize indexing
4. Which normalization form ensures that there are no transitive dependencies?
A) First Normal Form (1NF)
B) Second Normal Form (2NF)
C) Third Normal Form (3NF)
D) Boyce-Codd Normal Form (BCNF)
5. Which term describes an object or concept about which you want to store data?
A) Entity
B) Attribute
C) Tuple
D) Schema
6. What cardinality does a crow's foot notation with a single bar represent in an ER diagram?
A) One-to-One
B) One-to-Many

C) Many-to-One
D) Many-to-Many
7. Which normalization form eliminates partial dependencies?
A) First Normal Form (1NF)
B) Second Normal Form (2NF)
C) Third Normal Form (3NF)
D) Boyce-Codd Normal Form (BCNF)
8. Which design principle states that every column in a table should be dependent on the primary key?
A) Principle of Least Astonishment
B) Single Responsibility Principle
C) Law of Demeter
D) Domain-Key Normal Form (DKNF)
9. Which term describes a characteristic or property of an entity?
A) Entity
B) Attribute
C) Tuple
D) Schema
10. What cardinality does a crow's foot notation with three bars represent in an ER diagram?
A) One-to-One
B) One-to-Many
C) Many-to-One
D) Many-to-Many

Exercise 2 – True/ False

1. In data modeling, an ERD (Entity-Relationship Diagram) shows only entities and not the relationships between them.
2. An ERD represents the logical structure of a database and illustrates how data is related through entities and their relationships.
3. Normalization is the process of reducing redundancy and dependency by organizing fields and tables in a database.
4. Data modeling primarily focuses on the physical implementation of the database structure.
5. Denormalization is a design technique that often leads to improved database performance.
6. A relationship in an ERD can exist between entities of the same type.
7. Third Normal Form (3NF) allows for the existence of transitive dependencies.
8. Designing a database schema involves choosing appropriate data types for columns, considering storage requirements and data constraints.
9. Cardinality in an ERD specifies the maximum and minimum number of occurrences of one entity that may be related to a single occurrence of another entity.
10. Normalization aims to eliminate update anomalies by breaking large tables into smaller ones to reduce redundancy.

Exercise 3 – Fill in the blanks

1. Data modelling is the process of creating a __________ representation of the information used in an organization.
2. In an ERD, an entity is represented by a __________ shape.
3. The process of __________ reduces data redundancy and dependency by organizing fields and table structures.
4. Using __________ as primary keys in database design ensures unique identification of each record.
5. Relationships between entities are depicted using __________ lines in an ERD.
6. An ERD is an example of a __________ used to visually represent the structure of a database.
7. The process of __________ eliminates undesirable characteristics like insertion, update, and deletion anomalies.
8. __________ is a property that ensures each column in a table contains a single value.
9. In data modelling, a/an __________ defines the characteristics of an entity.
10. In normalization, the first normal form (1NF) ensures that each cell contains a __________.

Exercise 4 – One word answer

1. What is the process of representing real-world data in a structured format?
2. What graphical representation illustrates the relationships between entities in a database?
3. What process organizes a database to minimize redundancy and dependency?
4. What term refers to guidelines ensuring efficient and effective database structures?
5. What represents a distinct object or concept in a database?
6. What is a two-dimensional table that contains specific information?

7. What refers to the properties or characteristics of an entity?
8. What occurs when an attribute's value depends on another attribute?
9. What form ensures atomicity of values in a database?
10. What is a structured set of data stored electronically?

Exercise 5 – Small answer

1. Define data modeling and its significance in database development.
2. Explain the primary components depicted in an Entity-Relationship Diagram (ERD).
3. Briefly describe the purpose of normalization in database design.
4. Name the different normalization forms (up to 3NF) and briefly explain each.
5. Explain when and why denormalization might be used in a database.
6. Define what a primary key is and why it's important in a database table.
7. Describe the role of foreign keys in maintaining referential integrity.
8. Name two key principles of good database design and explain their significance.
9. Describe how normalization helps eliminate data redundancy and anomalies.
10. Explain two benefits of a highly normalized database structure.

Exercise 6 – Long answer

1. Explain the significance of data modeling in database design. Discuss the key phases involved in the data modeling process.
2. Detail the components of an Entity-Relationship Diagram (ERD) and their respective roles in modeling relationships between entities in a database.
3. Define normalization in the context of database design. Elaborate on the various normal forms and their objectives.
4. Discuss the best practices and principles that guide effective database design. Explain how these practices enhance performance, scalability, and maintainability.
5. Highlight the advantages and disadvantages of using a data modeling approach in designing and developing databases.
6. Outline the steps involved in creating an Entity-Relationship Diagram (ERD) for a complex business scenario. Emphasize the key considerations during the ERD development phase.
7. Explain the normalization process step by step. Describe each normalization form and its relevance in achieving a well-structured database.
8. Describe denormalization and its role in database design. Discuss the scenarios where denormalization is preferred and the strategies involved in its implementation.
9. Identify and elaborate on common pitfalls or mistakes encountered during the database design phase. Provide solutions or preventive measures to mitigate these issues.
10. Explore the trade-offs between database normalization and performance. Discuss how normalization can impact performance and strategies to maintain a balance between them.

Answer

Exercise 1:

Answer: 1: C, 2: C, 3: B, 4: C, 5: A, 6: A, 7: D, 8: D, 9: B, 10: D

Exercise 2:

Answer: 1: False, 2: True, 3: True, 4: False, 5: True, 6: True 7: False, 8: True, 9: True, 10: True

Exercise 3:

Answer: 1: graphical or diagrammatic,2: rectangular or square, 3: normalization, 4: surrogate keys, 5: connecting or linking, 6: diagram or model, 7: normalization, 8: atomicity, 9: attribute or property, 10: single or atomic value.

Exercise 4:

Answer: 1: Modeling,2: ERD, 3: Normalization, 4: Practices, 5: Entity, 6: Relation, 7: Attributes, 8: Dependency, 9: 1NF, 10: Database

ONLINE RESOURCES

Practice Paper

Link: https://forms.office.com/r/vcZFCFVbkG?origin=lprLink

QR Code:

Chapter 5: Working with Tables and Views

5.1 Constraints and Indexes

In Microsoft SQL Server, constraints and indexes play crucial roles in ensuring data integrity, optimizing query performance, and maintaining the database's efficiency. Here's a detailed overview with examples:

Constraints:

Primary Key Constraint:

Ensures uniqueness in a column or a set of columns and identifies each row uniquely within a table.

Example:

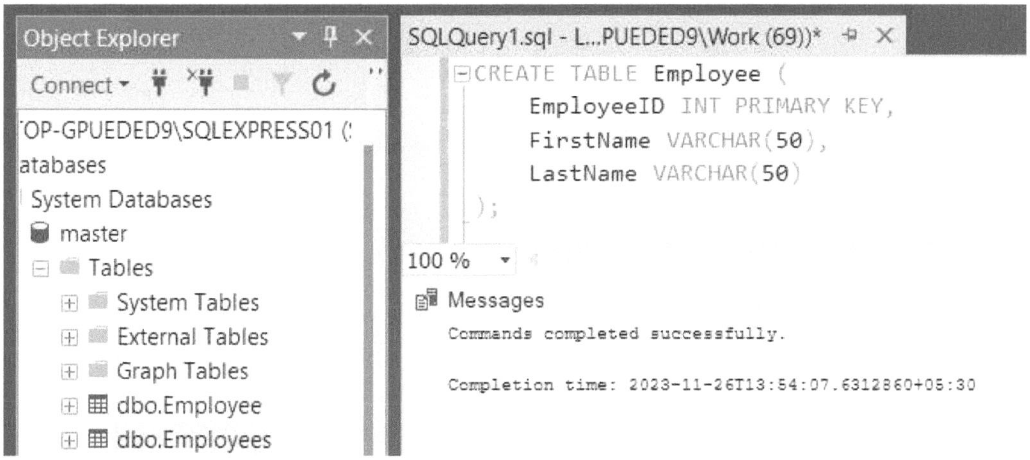

Foreign Key Constraint:

Maintains referential integrity between two tables by enforcing relationships.

Example:

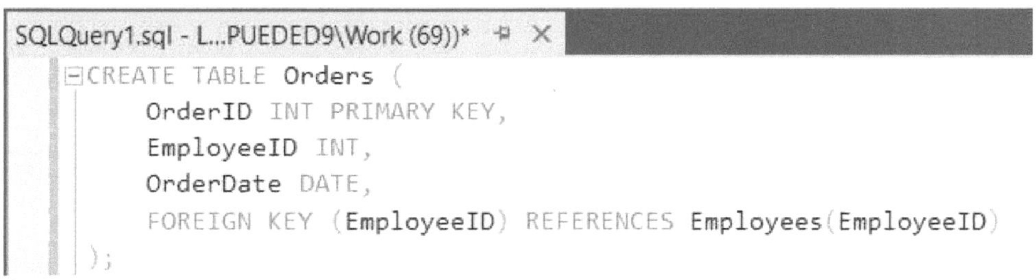

Unique Constraint:

Ensures uniqueness in a column or a set of columns, similar to the PRIMARY KEY constraint but allows NULL values.

Example:

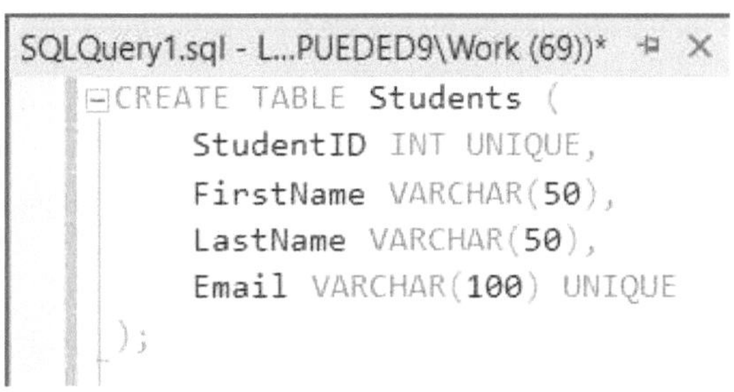

Check Constraint:

Imposes restrictions on the values that can be inserted into a column based on a Boolean expression.

Example:

```sql
CREATE TABLE Products (
    ProductID INT,
    ProductName VARCHAR(50),
    Quantity INT,
    CONSTRAINT CHK_Quantity CHECK (Quantity >= 0)
);
```

Indexes:

Clustered Index:

Defines the physical order of data in a table and is particularly useful for frequent range-based queries.

Example:

```sql
CREATE CLUSTERED INDEX IX_EmployeeID ON Employees(EmployeeID);
```

Non-Clustered Index:

Creates a separate structure that holds key values with pointers to the actual rows in the table.

Example:

```sql
CREATE NONCLUSTERED INDEX IX_LastName ON Employees(LastName);
```

Filtered Index:

Indexes a subset of rows in a table based on a filter condition, enhancing query performance.

Example:

```sql
CREATE INDEX IX_FilteredAge ON Employees(Age) WHERE Age >= 30;
```

Conclusion:

Constraints ensure data integrity by defining rules for permissible data values, relationships, and uniqueness. Indexes improve query performance by facilitating faster data retrieval through efficient data structures. Properly applying constraints and indexes based on the database design and usage patterns is essential for maintaining a well-optimized and consistent SQL Server database.

5.2 Creating and Using Views

In Microsoft SQL Server, views are virtual tables derived from the result set of a SELECT query. They provide a way to abstract complex queries, simplify data access, and enhance security by controlling access to certain columns or rows. Here's an overview of creating and using views with an example:

Creating a View:

To create a view, use the **CREATE VIEW** statement followed by a **SELECT** query:

```sql
CREATE VIEW vwEmployeeDetails
AS
SELECT
    EmployeeID,
    FirstName,
    LastName,
    DepartmentID
FROM
    Employees;
```

This creates a view named **vwEmployeeDetails** based on the **Employees** table, displaying only specific columns.

Using Views:

Views can be queried like tables, allowing users to retrieve data without needing direct access to the underlying tables:

Querying a View:

```sql
SELECT * FROM vwEmployeeDetails;
```

Applying Filters:

```sql
SELECT * FROM vwEmployeeDetails WHERE DepartmentID = 1;
```

Updatable Views:
Views can be updatable if they meet certain criteria (e.g., contain a single table and do not include certain constructs). Here's an example of an updatable view:

```sql
CREATE VIEW vwUpdatableEmployee AS
SELECT
    EmployeeID,.
    FirstName,
    LastName
FROM
    Employees
WHERE
    DepartmentID = 1;
```

Modifying Views:
To alter an existing view's definition:

```sql
ALTER VIEW vwEmployeeDetails
AS
SELECT
    EmployeeID,
    FirstName,
    LastName,
    DepartmentID,
    Email
FROM
    Employees;
```

Dropping Views:
Use **DROP VIEW** to remove a view:

```sql
DROP VIEW IF EXISTS vwEmployeeDetails;
```

Considerations:
Performance: Views don't store data; they execute the underlying query every time they are accessed, impacting performance for complex queries.
Security: Views can restrict access to certain columns or rows, enhancing security by limiting data visibility.
Abstraction: They abstract complex logic into simplified structures, aiding in code readability and maintenance.
Example Use Case:
Consider an HR database with an Employees table. A view **vwActiveEmployees** might display only active employees:

```sql
CREATE VIEW vwActiveEmployees
AS
SELECT
    EmployeeID,
    FirstName,
    LastName,
    DepartmentID
FROM
    Employees
WHERE
    IsActive = 1;
```

This view filters out inactive employees and provides a simplified list of active employees.
Conclusion:
Views in SQL Server offer a powerful way to abstract complex queries, control access to data, and simplify data retrieval. Their use should be strategic, considering the trade-offs between performance, security, and code manageability.

5.3 Temporary Tables and Table Variables

Temporary Tables:
Temporary tables are a type of table used to store temporary data that exists only for the duration of a session or a specific transaction.
Creating a Temporary Table:

```sql
-- Create a temporary table
CREATE TABLE #TempTable (
    ID INT,
    Name NVARCHAR(50)
);

-- Insert data into the temporary table
INSERT INTO #TempTable (ID, Name)
VALUES (1, 'John'), (2, 'Alice');

-- Select data from the temporary table
SELECT * FROM #TempTable;
```

Local vs. Global Temporary Tables:
Local Temporary Table (#TableName): Visible only within the current session and is automatically dropped when the session ends.
Global Temporary Table (##TableName): Visible to all sessions and is dropped when all sessions referencing the table are closed.
Example of Local and Global Temporary Tables:

```sql
-- Create a local temporary table
CREATE TABLE #LocalTempTable (
    ID INT,
    Name NVARCHAR(50)
);

-- Create a global temporary table
CREATE TABLE ##GlobalTempTable (
    ID INT,
    Name NVARCHAR(50)
);
```

Table Variables:
Table variables are variables that hold a table result set for use within a batch, procedure, or function.
Declaring and Using Table Variables:

```sql
-- Declare a table variable
DECLARE @TableVar TABLE (
    ID INT,
    Name NVARCHAR(50)
);

-- Insert data into the table variable
INSERT INTO @TableVar (ID, Name)
VALUES (1, 'Ram'), (2, 'Sham');

-- Select data from the table variable
SELECT * FROM @TableVar;
```

Differences Between Temporary Tables and Table Variables:
Scope: Temporary tables have a wider scope and can be used across sessions, while table variables are limited to the session or batch in which they are declared.
Transaction Log: Changes to table variables are not logged, unlike temporary tables which are logged.
Both temporary tables and table variables offer advantages based on specific requirements, and understanding their differences is crucial in selecting the appropriate tool for managing temporary data in SQL Server.

5.4 Exercise

Exercise 1 – MCQ

1. Which of the following best defines a primary key constraint in a database?
A) Allows null values in a unique column
B) Permits duplicate values in a column
C) Enforces uniqueness and identifies each row uniquely
D) Restricts the number of rows in a table
2. What is the purpose of an index in a database?
A) To define relationships between tables
B) To enforce data integrity constraints
C) To facilitate efficient data retrieval
D) To provide security to tables
3. In SQL, a view is:
A) A temporary table created at runtime
B) A physical table stored on disk
C) A stored query that behaves like a table

D) A table that exists only in memory
4. Which statement about views is true?
A) Views can be updated directly using INSERT, UPDATE, and DELETE statements.
B) Views can contain only SELECT statements.
C) Views cannot be joined with other tables.
D) Views are always stored physically as separate tables.
5. What differentiates a temporary table from a table variable in SQL Server?
A) Temporary tables are stored in the tempdb database, while table variables are stored in memory.
B) Table variables are stored in the tempdb database, while temporary tables are stored in memory.
C) Temporary tables are always accessible within a single session, while table variables are not.
D) Table variables can have constraints applied, while temporary tables cannot.
6. Which SQL command is used to create a temporary table in SQL Server?
A) CREATE TEMPORARY TABLE
B) DECLARE TABLE
C) CREATE TABLE #tablename
D) CREATE TABLE @tablename
7. What is the purpose of a foreign key constraint in a database?
A) It ensures unique values in a column.
B) It specifies default values for columns.
C) It maintains referential integrity between tables.
D) It enforces data type constraints.
8. Views can be used to:
A) Modify underlying table structures
B) Hide sensitive data from certain users
C) Perform complex mathematical calculations
D) Store large amounts of data temporarily
9. Which type of index is used to improve the performance of queries involving columns frequently used in WHERE clauses?
A) Clustered index
B) Non-clustered index
C) Unique index
D) Bitmap index
10. Which of the following statements is true about table variables in SQL Server?
A) Table variables can be dropped using the DROP TABLE statement.
B) Table variables can have triggers associated with them.
C) Table variables are automatically dropped at the end of the transaction.
D) Table variables can be shared across multiple sessions.

Exercise 2 – True/ False
1. A primary key constraint can consist of multiple columns in a table.
2. Indexes are primarily used for maintaining the physical order of rows in a table.
3. Views in a database are always physically stored as a separate set of data from the original tables.
4. A view allows updates to be made on the underlying tables only through the view itself.
5. Temporary tables are visible to other users in the database by default.
6. Table variables are stored in the tempdb database similar to temporary tables.
7. A unique constraint and a unique index are functionally the same and have identical internal implementations.
8. Views can be indexed to improve performance in certain query scenarios.
9. Table variables can have constraints such as primary keys or foreign keys defined on them.
10. A clustered index determines the physical order of data in a table, while a non-clustered index does not affect the physical order of data.

Exercise 3 – Fill in the blanks
1. Constraints ensure __________ and maintain __________ integrity in a database.
2. An index in a database is utilized to speed up the __________ operation.
3. Views in SQL provide a way to present a __________ perspective of the data stored in one or more tables.

4. Temporary tables are visible only to the __________ that creates them and are dropped automatically when the __________ session ends.
5. Table variables are created using the DECLARE statement and exist for the duration of the __________.
6. Constraints like __________ guarantee that every value in a column is unique.
7. An index on a table can be created using the __________ statement.
8. Views can simplify __________ by abstracting complex joins or calculations into a single virtual table.
9. Temporary tables are useful for __________ data that needs to be manipulated or processed temporarily.
10. Table variables are typically used when only a small amount of __________ is stored temporarily.

Exercise 4 – One word answer
1. What enforces data integrity rules in a table?
2. What provides a virtual representation of data based on a SELECT query?
3. What are used to store temporary data within a session or a specific scope?
4. What uniquely identifies each record in a table?
5. What physically sorts and stores table records based on the index key?
6. What are precomputed and stored physically, unlike regular views?
7. What doesn't affect the physical order of the table rows?
8. What is accessible to all users and is dropped when the session ends?
9. What ensures that values in a column are unique, except for NULLs?
10. What is a view with a unique clustered index created on it?

Exercise 5 – Small answer
1. Define and explain the purpose of constraints in SQL databases. Provide examples of different types of constraints.
2. What are indexes in a database? Describe the types of indexes available in SQL and their significance in query optimization.
3. Explain what a view is in SQL. How does it differ from a table? Provide an example of when and why views are commonly used.
4. Discuss the syntax and process of creating a view in SQL. Highlight the benefits of using views in database management.
5. Can views be modified after creation? Explain the possibilities and limitations associated with altering views in SQL.
6. What are temporary tables, and how are they used in SQL? Provide scenarios where temporary tables prove advantageous.
7. Differentiate between temporary tables and table variables. When would you opt for a table variable over a temporary table?
8. Discuss the role of constraints in table creation. How do constraints ensure data integrity and reliability?
9. How do indexes impact query performance? Describe situations where indexes significantly enhance query execution.
10. Explain how views contribute to database security. Can views restrict access to sensitive data in a database? Provide examples.

Exercise 6 – Long answer
1. Explain the significance of constraints in database tables. Discuss the types of constraints available in SQL Server and how they enforce data integrity.
2. Elaborate on the purpose of indexes in database tables. Discuss different types of indexes and their impact on query performance and database operations.
3. Describe the concept of views in SQL Server. How are they created, and what advantages do they offer in managing data retrieval and security?
4. Compare and contrast materialized views and regular views. Discuss their functionalities, differences in storage mechanisms, and scenarios where each type is beneficial.
5. Explain the use of temporary tables in SQL Server. Describe their types, lifespan, and situations where they prove beneficial during data operations.
6. Discuss the differences between table variables and temporary tables. Explain their scope, behavior, and performance implications in SQL Server.
7. Illustrate how various constraints like primary key, foreign key, and check constraints are applied practically in table creation, using real-world examples.

8. Explore advanced indexing techniques, such as covering indexes or filtered indexes, and their impact on query performance and storage requirements.
9. Detail strategies for optimizing view performance in SQL Server. Discuss techniques like indexed views or view partitioning to enhance query execution.
10. Discuss the role of temporary tables within transaction management. Explain how they behave within transactional boundaries and their impact on data consistency.

Answer

Exercise 1:
Answer: 1: C, 2: C, 3: C, 4: B, 5: A, 6: C, 7: C, 8: B, 9: B, 10: C

Exercise 2:
Answer: 1: True, 2: False, 3: False, 4: True, 5: False, 6: True 7: True, 8: False, 9: False, 10: True

Exercise 3:
Answer: 1: data integrity, referential ,2: data retrieval, 3: virtual, 4: session, session, 5: batch, 6: UNIQUE, 7: CREATE INDEX, 8: queries, 9: staging, 10: data

Exercise 4:
Answer: 1: Constraints, 2: Views, 3: TempTables, 4: Primary, 5: Clustered, 6: Materialized, 7: NonClustered, 8: Global, 9: Unique, 10: IndexedView.

ONLINE RESOURCES

Practice Paper
Link: https://forms.office.com/r/wEH83TXfXx?origin=lprLink
QR Code:

Chapter 6: Stored Procedures, Functions, and Triggers

6.1 Creating and Managing Stored Procedures

Creating and managing stored procedures in Microsoft SQL Server allows for encapsulating logic, enhancing security, and improving performance. Here's a detailed guide along with an example:

Creating a Stored Procedure:

Syntax:

```
CREATE PROCEDURE procedure_name
   @parameter1 datatype1,
   @parameter2 datatype2,
   ...
AS
BEGIN
   -- SQL statements
END
```

Example:

Let's create a simple stored procedure that retrieves employee details based on a department ID.

```
CREATE PROCEDURE GetEmployeesByDepartmentID
    @DeptID INT
AS
BEGIN
    SELECT EmployeeID, FirstName, LastName
    FROM Employees
    WHERE DepartmentID = @DeptID;
END
```

Executing a Stored Procedure:

Syntax:

```
EXEC procedure_name parameter_values;
```

Example:

Execute the **GetEmployeesByDepartmentID** procedure:

```
EXEC GetEmployeesByDepartmentID @DeptID = 3;
```

Managing Stored Procedures:

Altering a Stored Procedure:

To modify an existing stored procedure, use the **ALTER PROCEDURE** statement followed by the changes.

Example:

Alter the previous stored procedure to include the email:

```
ALTER PROCEDURE GetEmployeesByDepartmentID
    @DeptID INT
AS
BEGIN
    SELECT EmployeeID, FirstName, LastName, Email
    FROM Employees
    WHERE DepartmentID = @DeptID;
END
```

Dropping a Stored Procedure:

To remove a stored procedure, use the **DROP PROCEDURE** statement.

Example:

Drop the **GetEmployeesByDepartmentID** procedure:

```sql
DROP PROCEDURE GetEmployeesByDepartmentID;
```

Advantages of Stored Procedures:
Performance: Pre-compiled execution plans improve performance.
Security: Control access and permissions to database objects.
Modularity: Encapsulate logic for reuse and maintainability.
Reduced Network Traffic: Execute complex operations on the server, reducing data transfer.
Considerations:
Parameters: Use parameters for flexibility and security, preventing SQL injection.
Error Handling: Implement error handling within procedures to manage exceptions.
Optimization: Regularly review and optimize stored procedures for improved performance.
Stored procedures in SQL Server offer significant advantages in managing and optimizing database operations. Utilize them judiciously based on the specific needs of your application for enhanced security, performance, and maintainability.

6.2 User-Defined Functions (UDFs)

User-Defined Functions (UDFs) in Microsoft SQL Server allow you to create custom functions to encapsulate specific logic and perform computations, which can be reused across queries. There are three types of UDFs: Scalar, Inline Table-Valued, and Multi-Statement Table-Valued.
Scalar UDFs:
Scalar functions return a single value based on the input parameters.
Example:

```sql
CREATE FUNCTION dbo.CalculateDiscount(@price DECIMAL(10, 2), @discountPercentage DECIMAL(5, 2))
RETURNS DECIMAL(10, 2)
AS
BEGIN
    DECLARE @discount DECIMAL(10, 2);
    SET @discount = @price * (@discountPercentage / 100.0);
    RETURN @discount;
END;
```

Usage:

```sql
SELECT dbo.CalculateDiscount(100, 10) AS DiscountAmount;
```

Inline Table-Valued Functions (Inline TVFs):
Inline TVFs return a table result based on input parameters.
Example:

```sql
CREATE FUNCTION dbo.GetEmployeesByDepartment(@deptID INT)
RETURNS TABLE
AS
RETURN
(
    SELECT * FROM Employees WHERE DepartmentID = @deptID
);
```

Usage:

```sql
SELECT * FROM dbo.GetEmployeesByDepartment(2);
```

Multi-Statement Table-Valued Functions (Multi-ST TVFs):
Multi-ST TVFs return a table result through a defined set of statements.
Example:

```sql
CREATE FUNCTION dbo.GetEmployeesWithSalaryAbove(@salary DECIMAL(10, 2))
RETURNS @EmployeesAboveSalary TABLE (
    EmployeeID INT,
    FirstName NVARCHAR(50),
    LastName NVARCHAR(50)
)
AS
BEGIN
    INSERT INTO @EmployeesAboveSalary
    SELECT EmployeeID, FirstName, LastName FROM Employees WHERE Salary > @salary;
    RETURN;
END;
```

Usage:

```sql
SELECT * FROM dbo.GetEmployeesWithSalaryAbove(50000);
```

Considerations:

Performance: Be cautious with UDFs in queries as they can impact query performance, especially when used in larger datasets or complex queries.

Scalability: Use UDFs judiciously to avoid unnecessary complexity in queries.

Modularity: UDFs enhance code modularity and reusability but overusing them can lead to maintenance challenges.

Conclusion:

UDFs in SQL Server offer a powerful way to encapsulate logic for reuse, but their performance impact should be considered. Choose the appropriate type of function based on the specific requirements of your queries and aim for a balance between code modularity and query performance.

6.3 Triggers and Their Applications

Triggers in Microsoft SQL Server are special types of stored procedures that automatically execute in response to certain events occurring in the database. They are powerful tools for enforcing data integrity, implementing business rules, and maintaining consistency. Let's explore triggers and their applications in SQL Server with an example:

Types of Triggers:

After Triggers (AFTER INSERT, UPDATE, DELETE): Executed after the triggering event (e.g., after an insert, update, or delete operation).

Instead of Triggers: Substitutes the original operation with the trigger code.

Applications of Triggers:

Auditing and Logging Changes:

Create triggers to log changes made to critical tables, allowing you to track modifications for auditing purposes.

Example:

Consider a scenario where an audit trail is needed for changes to the Employees table:

```sql
CREATE TABLE EmployeeAudit (
    AuditID INT IDENTITY(1,1) PRIMARY KEY,
    EmployeeID INT,
    AuditDate DATETIME,
    Operation VARCHAR(10)
);

CREATE TRIGGER trg_AuditChanges
ON Employees
AFTER INSERT, UPDATE, DELETE
AS
BEGIN
    IF EXISTS (SELECT * FROM inserted)
    BEGIN
        INSERT INTO EmployeeAudit (EmployeeID, AuditDate, Operation)
        SELECT EmployeeID, GETDATE(), 'INSERT'
        FROM inserted;
    END;

    IF EXISTS (SELECT * FROM deleted)
    BEGIN
        INSERT INTO EmployeeAudit (EmployeeID, AuditDate, Operation)
        SELECT EmployeeID, GETDATE(), 'DELETE'
        FROM deleted;
    END;
END;
```

This trigger creates an **EmployeeAudit** table to track operations (INSERT, DELETE) on the **Employees** table.
Enforcing Business Rules:
Use triggers to enforce specific business rules, validations, or constraints that cannot be handled by traditional constraints.
Example:
Implement a trigger to ensure that employee salaries do not exceed a certain limit:

```sql
CREATE TRIGGER trg_CheckSalaryLimit
ON Employees
AFTER INSERT, UPDATE
AS
BEGIN
    IF EXISTS (SELECT 1 FROM inserted WHERE Salary > 100000)
    BEGIN
        RAISERROR ('Salary limit exceeded!', 16, 1);
        ROLLBACK TRANSACTION;
    END;
END;
```

This trigger prevents salary updates or inserts that exceed the defined limit.
Complex Data Modifications:
Perform additional complex data modifications or cascading updates based on specific conditions using triggers.

Example:
Automatically update related tables when an employee's department changes:

```
CREATE TRIGGER trg_UpdateRelatedData
ON Employees
AFTER UPDATE
AS
BEGIN
    IF UPDATE(DepartmentID)
    BEGIN
        UPDATE OtherTable
        SET SomeColumn = 'Updated'
        FROM OtherTable OT
        INNER JOIN inserted I ON OT.EmployeeID = I.EmployeeID;
    END;
END;
```

This trigger updates data in another table (**OtherTable**) associated with the modified employee.

Conclusion:

Triggers in SQL Server offer a versatile means to enforce rules, maintain data integrity, and automate actions based on database changes. However, excessive use of triggers can make the database complex, so it's essential to use them judiciously and document their purpose clearly.

6.4 Error Handling and Transactions

In Microsoft SQL Server, error handling and transactions are crucial for maintaining data integrity and handling unexpected issues that might occur during database operations. Here's a breakdown of error handling and transactions:

Error Handling:

TRY...CATCH Block:

The TRY...CATCH block is used to handle exceptions within SQL Server.

```
BEGIN TRY
    -- SQL statements that might cause an error
    SELECT 1 / 0; -- Example division by zero
END TRY
BEGIN CATCH
    -- Error handling code
    SELECT ERROR_NUMBER() AS ErrorNumber, ERROR_MESSAGE() AS ErrorMessage;
END CATCH;
```

BEGIN TRY and **END TRY**: Encloses the code block where errors might occur.

BEGIN CATCH and **END CATCH**: Catches and handles exceptions thrown in the try block.

Error Functions:

ERROR_NUMBER(): Returns the error number.

ERROR_MESSAGE(): Returns the error description.

Transactions:

BEGIN TRANSACTION, COMMIT, ROLLBACK:

Transactions ensure that a series of database operations are executed as a single unit. If any part fails, the entire transaction can be rolled back to maintain data consistency.

```sql
BEGIN TRANSACTION;
    -- SQL statements
    INSERT INTO Employees (Name, Salary) VALUES ('John', 50000);
    UPDATE Departments SET Budget = Budget - 10000 WHERE DepartmentID = 1;

COMMIT TRANSACTION; -- If successful
-- ROLLBACK TRANSACTION; -- If an error occurs
```

BEGIN TRANSACTION: Starts a new transaction.
COMMIT TRANSACTION: Saves changes made within the transaction to the database.
ROLLBACK TRANSACTION: Undoes all changes made within the transaction and returns to the start.
SAVEPOINT:
Savepoints help in implementing partial rollback within a transaction.

```sql
BEGIN TRANSACTION;
    INSERT INTO Table1 VALUES (1, 'Value1');
    SAVE TRANSACTION Savepoint1;
    INSERT INTO Table2 VALUES (2, 'Value2');
    IF @@ERROR <> 0 ROLLBACK TRANSACTION Savepoint1;
COMMIT TRANSACTION;
```

SAVE TRANSACTION: Creates a savepoint within the transaction.
Example:

```sql
BEGIN TRY
    BEGIN TRANSACTION;
        INSERT INTO Employees (Name, Salary) VALUES ('Alice', 60000);
        UPDATE Departments SET Budget = Budget - 15000 WHERE DepartmentID = 2;
    COMMIT TRANSACTION;
END TRY
BEGIN CATCH
    IF @@TRANCOUNT > 0
        ROLLBACK TRANSACTION;
    SELECT ERROR_NUMBER() AS ErrorNumber, ERROR_MESSAGE() AS ErrorMessage;
END CATCH;
```

The **TRY...CATCH** block wraps the transaction, ensuring that if an error occurs, the transaction is rolled back to maintain data integrity.
Conclusion:
Error handling using **TRY...CATCH** allows for graceful handling of exceptions, while transactions (**BEGIN TRANSACTION**, **COMMIT**, **ROLLBACK**, **SAVE TRANSACTION**) ensure that operations are performed atomically, helping maintain the database's consistency and recoverability in case of errors. Always wrap critical operations within transactions and implement robust error handling for reliable database operations.

6.5 Exercise

Exercise 1 – MCQ

1. Which of the following is true about stored procedures?
A) They cannot return values.
B) They always return a single value.
C) They can return multiple result sets.
D) They cannot accept parameters.
2. Which type of User-Defined Function does not allow data modification?

A) Scalar Functions
B) Inline Table-Valued Functions
C) Multi-statement Table-Valued Functions
D) Aggregate Functions
3. What is the main purpose of a trigger in SQL Server?
A) To perform complex calculations
B) To enforce data integrity rules
C) To create temporary tables
D) To execute recursive queries
4. In SQL Server, which statement is used to handle errors within stored procedures or T-SQL blocks?
A) TRY...CATCH
B) IF...ELSE
C) SELECT...CASE
D) BEGIN...END
5. Which keyword is used to begin a transaction in SQL Server?
A) BEGIN TRANSACTION
B) COMMIT TRANSACTION
C) START TRANSACTION
D) INITIATE TRANSACTION
6. Which SQL command is used to create a stored procedure in SQL Server?
A) CREATE FUNCTION
B) CREATE PROCEDURE
C) CREATE TRIGGER
D) CREATE TABLE
7. Which type of User-Defined Function returns a table?
A) Scalar Functions
B) Inline Table-Valued Functions
C) Multi-statement Table-Valued Functions
D) Aggregate Functions
8. In SQL Server, which trigger type fires automatically after an INSERT, UPDATE, or DELETE operation?
A) INSTEAD OF trigger
B) AFTER trigger
C) BEFORE trigger
D) FOR trigger
9. What is RAISEERROR used for in SQL Server?
A) To handle exceptions
B) To raise a system error message
C) To rollback a transaction
D) To handle arithmetic errors
10. Which SQL statement is used to permanently save the changes made by a transaction in SQL Server?
A) BEGIN TRANSACTION
B) ROLLBACK TRANSACTION
C) COMMIT TRANSACTION
D) END TRANSACTION

Exercise 2 – True/ False

1. Stored Procedures can return values using output parameters or result sets.
2. UDFs are limited to performing read-only operations and cannot modify data.
3. Triggers are associated with tables and cannot be directly applied to views.
4. These blocks provide structured error handling in T-SQL.
5. Transactions help maintain data consistency by either committing all changes or rolling back in case of errors.
6. Stored Procedures are compiled once and stored in a compiled format for faster execution.
7. Triggers can execute after INSERT, UPDATE, and DELETE operations.
8. UDFs are not allowed to modify the database schema.
9. TRY...CATCH blocks can handle a variety of error conditions.
10. SQL Server does not support nested transactions, although nested TRY...CATCH blocks are allowed.

Exercise 3 – Fill in the blanks

1. __________ allow us to store T-SQL statements for later execution.
2. User-Defined Functions (UDFs) can be either __________ or __________.
3. Triggers are database objects that automatically perform actions based on __________.
4. A trigger defined to execute after an INSERT operation is known as an __________ trigger.
5. Transactions in SQL ensure that a series of operations are treated as a single __________ unit.
6. __________ provide a way to handle errors in T-SQL code.
7. The __________ keyword is used in SQL Server to begin a transaction.
8. The __________ statement rolls back a transaction.
9. In SQL Server, the __________ function is used to obtain the last error message.
10. A __________ allows you to execute a block of code in response to a specific event occurring in the database.

Exercise 5 – One word answer

1. What are Stored Procedures?
2. What do UDFs stand for?
3. What are used to perform actions in response to specific events?
4. Handling unexpected situations in SQL is known as what?
5. What do transactions ensure in SQL?
6. What do you call grouping multiple SQL statements together?
7. What enables rollbacks in SQL transactions?
8. What ensures atomicity, consistency, isolation, and durability?
9. What is used to control the flow of execution in stored procedures?
10. What improves database performance by reducing network traffic?

Exercise 6 – Small answer

1. Define a stored procedure in SQL Server.
2. How do you call a stored procedure from within another stored procedure?
3. What are the advantages of using stored procedures?
4. When do triggers get executed in the database?
5. Provide an example scenario where triggers might be used.

Exercise 7 – Long answer

1. Explain the process of creating and managing stored procedures in SQL Server. Discuss their significance in enhancing database management and application performance.
2. Define triggers in SQL Server and elucidate their role in maintaining data integrity. Discuss various trigger types and scenarios where they are beneficial.
3. Explain the concept of transactions in SQL Server and their role in ensuring data consistency. Elaborate on ACID properties and the types of transactions.
4. Discuss the advantages and disadvantages of using UDFs in SQL Server. Provide examples of scenarios where UDFs are preferred or discouraged.
5. Explore advanced error handling techniques, such as using nested TRY...CATCH blocks or handling specific error types. Discuss their applicability and considerations.

Answer

Exercise 1:

Answer: 1: C, 2: A, 3: B, 4: A, 5: A, 6: D, 7: B, 8: B, 9: B, 10: C

Exercise 2:

Answer: 1: False, 2: True, 3: True, 4: True, 5: True, 6: False, 7: False, 8: False, 9: False, 10: False

Exercise 3:

Answer: 1: Stored Procedures, 2: Scalar, Table-valued, 3: Certain events (like INSERT, UPDATE, DELETE), 4: AFTER, 5: Atomic, 6: TRY...CATCH blocks, 7: BEGIN TRANSACTION, 8: ROLLBACK, 9: ERROR_MESSAGE(), 10: Trigger.

Exercise 4:

Answer: 1: Procedures, 2: Functions, 3: Triggers, 4: Error, 5: Consistency, 6: Batching, 7: Undo, 8: ACID, 9: Control, 10: Cursor.

ONLINE RESOURCES

Practice Paper
Link: https://forms.office.com/r/jMHuh4ftR4?origin=lprLink
QR Code:

Chapter 7: Managing Data with T-SQL

7.1 Managing Data with T-SQL

Managing data with Transact-SQL (T-SQL) in Microsoft SQL Server involves several key aspects. Here's an overview with examples:

Data Manipulation Language (DML)

T-SQL provides commands for data manipulation within SQL Server databases.

Example:

```
-- Inserting Data
INSERT INTO Employees (FirstName, LastName, Age, Department)
VALUES ('John', 'Doe', 30, 'IT');

-- Updating Data
UPDATE Employees
SET Age = 31
WHERE LastName = 'Doe';

-- Deleting Data
DELETE FROM Employees
WHERE FirstName = 'John';
```

Data Querying with SELECT

SELECT statements are used to retrieve data from SQL Server tables.

Example:

```
-- Retrieving Data
SELECT FirstName, LastName, Age
FROM Employees
WHERE Department = 'IT';
```

Transactions and Error Handling

T-SQL allows transactions to ensure data integrity and error handling to manage exceptions.

Example:

```
BEGIN TRANSACTION;
BEGIN TRY
    INSERT INTO Employees (FirstName, LastName, Age, Department)
    VALUES ('Alice', 'Smith', 28, 'HR');
    COMMIT TRANSACTION;
END TRY
BEGIN CATCH
    ROLLBACK TRANSACTION;
    PRINT ERROR_MESSAGE();
END CATCH;
```

Stored Procedures

T-SQL supports creating stored procedures, which are precompiled sets of SQL statements stored in the database.

Example:

```sql
-- Creating a Stored Procedure
CREATE PROCEDURE GetEmployeeDetails
    @DeptName NVARCHAR(50)
AS
BEGIN
    SELECT FirstName, LastName, Age
    FROM Employees
    WHERE Department = @DeptName;
END;
```

Functions

Functions in T-SQL allow encapsulating logic and returning specific values.

Example:

```sql
-- Creating a Function
CREATE FUNCTION CalculateBonus (@Salary MONEY)
RETURNS MONEY
AS
BEGIN
    DECLARE @Bonus MONEY;
    SET @Bonus = @Salary * 0.1; -- Assuming 10% bonus
    RETURN @Bonus;
END;
```

Cursors

T-SQL Cursors allow row-by-row processing of query results.

Example:

```sql
DECLARE @FirstName NVARCHAR(50);
DECLARE cursor_name CURSOR FOR
SELECT FirstName FROM Employees;

OPEN cursor_name;
FETCH NEXT FROM cursor_name INTO @FirstName;

WHILE @@FETCH_STATUS = 0
BEGIN
    PRINT @FirstName;
    FETCH NEXT FROM cursor_name INTO @FirstName;
END;

CLOSE cursor_name;
DEALLOCATE cursor_name;
```

These examples cover some fundamental aspects of managing data with T-SQL in SQL Server, showcasing data manipulation, querying, transactions, stored procedures, functions, and cursors.

7.2 Bulk Operations

Bulk operations in Microsoft SQL Server refer to performing large-scale insertions, updates, or deletions efficiently. These operations are critical for managing substantial amounts of data. Here's an overview with examples:

Bulk Insertions:

Bulk insertions involve adding large volumes of data into tables using minimal resources. SQL Server offers the **BULK INSERT** statement for this purpose.

Example:

```
BULK INSERT dbo.Employee
FROM 'C:\EmployeeData.csv'
WITH (FIELDTERMINATOR = ',', ROWTERMINATOR = '\n', BATCHSIZE = 1000)
```

Explanation:

BULK INSERT is used to load data from the specified CSV file into the **Employee** table.

FIELDTERMINATOR specifies the delimiter in the CSV file.

ROWTERMINATOR specifies the end-of-line character.

BATCHSIZE controls the number of rows processed in each batch.

Bulk Updates:

Bulk updates modify large sets of data efficiently. One way to perform this is using the **UPDATE** statement with joins or subqueries.

Example:

```
UPDATE Products
SET Price = Price * 1.1
WHERE CategoryID IN (SELECT CategoryID FROM Categories WHERE CategoryName = 'Electronics')
```

Explanation:

This query increases the price of products in the 'Electronics' category by 10%.

Bulk Deletions:

Bulk deletions remove large amounts of data from tables without affecting server performance. It uses the **DELETE** statement.

Example:

```
DELETE FROM Orders
WHERE OrderDate < '2022-01-01'
```

Explanation:

This query deletes orders placed before January 1, 2022.

Bulk Operations in Transactions:

Bulk operations can be encapsulated within transactions for data integrity. Begin a transaction, perform bulk operations, and commit or roll back accordingly.

Example:

```
BEGIN TRANSACTION
BULK INSERT dbo.TempData
FROM 'C:\TempData.csv'
COMMIT TRANSACTION
```

Explanation:

Begins a transaction, performs a bulk insertion from a CSV file into a temporary table, and commits the transaction. Using bulk operations is advantageous for efficiency and reduced resource consumption when handling large datasets in Microsoft SQL Server.

7.3 Working with XML Data

Working with XML data in Microsoft SQL Server involves storing, querying, and manipulating XML-based information within the database. Here's an overview with examples:

Storing XML Data:

XML data can be stored in SQL Server columns with the **XML** data type. For instance, creating a table with an XML column:

```
CREATE TABLE XmlData (
    Id INT PRIMARY KEY,
    XmlContent XML
);

INSERT INTO XmlData (Id, XmlContent)
VALUES (1, '<Person><Name>Ram</Name><Age>30</Age></Person>');
```

Querying XML Data:

Extracting Values:

```
SELECT XmlContent.value('(Person/Name)[1]', 'VARCHAR(50)') AS Name,
       XmlContent.value('(Person/Age)[1]', 'INT') AS Age
FROM XmlData;
```

Modifying XML:

```
UPDATE XmlData
SET XmlContent.modify('
    replace value of (Person/Age/text())[1]
    with "31"
')
WHERE Id = 1;
```

Indexing XML Data:

Creating an XML index on an XML column to improve query performance:

```
CREATE PRIMARY XML INDEX XmlIndex ON XmlData(XmlContent);
```

Handling XML Schemas:

Defining an XML schema collection:

```
CREATE XML SCHEMA COLLECTION XmlSchema AS
N'<?xml version="1.0"?>
<xs:schema xmlns:xs="http://www.w3.org/2001/XMLSchema">
    <xs:element name="Person">
        <xs:complexType>
            <xs:sequence>
                <xs:element name="Name" type="xs:string"/>
                <xs:element name="Age" type="xs:int"/>
            </xs:sequence>
        </xs:complexType>
    </xs:element>
</xs:schema>';
```

Working with XML Functions:

Existence Check:

```sql
SELECT Id, XmlContent.exist('/Person/Address') AS HasAddress
FROM XmlData;
```

Shredding XML into Rows:

```sql
SELECT Id, Person.value('(Name)[1]', 'VARCHAR(50)') AS Name,
           Person.value('(Age)[1]', 'INT') AS Age
FROM XmlData
CROSS APPLY XmlContent.nodes('/Person') AS Tbl(Person);
```

Use Cases:

Data Exchange: XML is used to exchange structured data between different systems.

Configuration Files: Storing configuration settings in XML format.

Web Services: Communicating data between web services using XML-based messages.

Working with XML in SQL Server enables handling semi-structured data efficiently, facilitating diverse scenarios like data integration and information interchange in various formats.

7.4 Dynamic SQL and Cursors

Dynamic SQL:

Dynamic SQL refers to generating SQL statements dynamically during runtime, allowing for flexibility in constructing queries based on changing conditions or user input. It involves building SQL statements as strings and then executing them.

Example:

```sql
DECLARE @ColumnName NVARCHAR(50) = 'ProductID'
DECLARE @SQLQuery NVARCHAR(MAX)
SET @SQLQuery = 'SELECT ' + QUOTENAME(@ColumnName) + ' FROM Products'
EXEC sp_executesql @SQLQuery
```

Cursors:

Cursors in SQL Server are database objects used to traverse a result set row by row. They provide a way to process individual rows for complex logic, but they can impact performance and should be used judiciously.

Example:

```sql
DECLARE @ProductName NVARCHAR(50)
DECLARE ProductCursor CURSOR FOR
SELECT ProductName FROM Products
OPEN ProductCursor
FETCH NEXT FROM ProductCursor INTO @ProductName
WHILE @@FETCH_STATUS = 0
BEGIN
    -- Perform operations on each ProductName
    PRINT @ProductName
    FETCH NEXT FROM ProductCursor INTO @ProductName
END
CLOSE ProductCursor
DEALLOCATE ProductCursor
```

These examples illustrate the basic usage of Dynamic SQL and Cursors in SQL Server. Dynamic SQL offers flexibility but requires careful handling to prevent SQL injection vulnerabilities. Cursors provide row-level processing but may impact performance, so alternative set-based approaches are often preferred for efficiency.

7.5 Exercise

Exercise 1 – MCQ

1. Which statement is used in T-SQL to add a new record to a table?
a) UPDATE
b) INSERT
c) DELETE
d) SELECT
2. Q: Which command in T-SQL is commonly used for inserting large batches of data efficiently?
a) BULK INSERT
b) INSERT INTO
c) MERGE
d) UPDATE
3. Which T-SQL function is used to extract a specific value from an XML data type?
a) XML PATH
b) XML VALUE
c) XML EXTRACT
d) XML QUERY
4. Which type of cursor in SQL Server allows navigating forward only through the result set?
a) Dynamic
b) Static
c) Forward-Only
d) Scroll
5. Which clause is used to filter records in a SELECT statement based on specific conditions?
a) ORDER BY
b) GROUP BY
c) WHERE
d) HAVING
6. Which T-SQL statement is used to remove all records from a table without deleting the table structure?
a) TRUNCATE TABLE
b) DROP TABLE
c) DELETE TABLE
d) CLEAR TABLE
7. In XML data type, what is the purpose of the nodes() method?
a) Extracts attributes from XML
b) Extracts elements from XML
c) Performs node comparison
d) Converts XML to string
8. Which T-SQL construct is used to execute a dynamically built SQL statement?
a) OPEN CURSOR
b) EXECUTE
c) RUN SQL
d) PERFORM
9. Which T-SQL statement is used to modify existing records in a table?
a) ADD
b) ALTER
c) UPDATE
d) MODIFY
10. Which statement is true about the MERGE statement in SQL Server?
a) It can only perform insert operations.
b) It performs a combination of insert, update, and delete operations.
c) It is used for bulk deleting of records.
d) It exclusively updates existing records.

Exercise 2 – True/ False

1. T-SQL provides tools and commands for managing data within SQL Server databases.

2. Bulk operations in SQL Server allow the processing of large volumes of data in smaller transactions for improved performance.
3. SQL Server supports native handling of XML data, allowing storage, retrieval, and manipulation of XML documents.
4. Dynamic SQL enables the creation and execution of SQL statements at runtime, offering flexibility but potentially raising security concerns.
5. T-SQL is primarily used for managing hardware resources and system-level processes in SQL Server.
6. Bulk operations are suitable for performing row-by-row processing in SQL Server databases.
7. SQL Server lacks support for parsing and querying XML data stored within database tables.
8. Cursors in SQL Server are preferred for processing large result sets efficiently.
9. T-SQL enables data modification through commands like INSERT, UPDATE, and DELETE.
10. Bulk operations can significantly enhance performance when inserting large volumes of data into SQL Server tables.

Exercise 3 – Fill in the blanks

1. T-SQL provides commands like __________ and __________ for data manipulation in SQL Server.
2. Bulk operations in SQL Server, like __________, allow efficient loading of large datasets into a database.
3. The __________ function in SQL Server facilitates the transformation of SQL query results into XML format.
4. Dynamic SQL is used to construct SQL statements __________, while cursors are used to __________ through a result set.
5. The __________ statement is used to remove rows from a table in SQL Server.
6. When performing bulk operations, the __________ command allows you to copy data from a file into a SQL Server table.
7. SQL Server provides the __________ function, which transforms XML data into tabular format for querying.
8. __________ allows SQL statements to be constructed dynamically based on variables or conditions.
9. The __________ statement in SQL is used to add new rows of data into a table.
10. The __________ utility is a command-line tool used for importing or exporting data in and out of SQL Server.

Exercise 4 – One word answer

1. What does T-SQL stand for?
2. What utility allows importing large volumes of data efficiently into SQL Server?
3. What data type is used to store XML data in SQL Server?
4. What SQL feature enables generating SQL statements dynamically at runtime?
5.Which SQL statement is used to modify existing records in a table?
6. What is the purpose of the BULK INSERT statement?
7. What is the FOR-XML clause used for in SQL Server?
8.What is a cursor in SQL?
9. What is the purpose of the DELETE statement in SQL?
10. Name one method to perform bulk operations in SQL Server besides BULK INSERT.

Exercise 5 – Small answer

1. Explain the significance of T-SQL in managing data within SQL Server. Provide three essential T-SQL statements used for data manipulation.
2. Define bulk operations in SQL Server. Name two commands utilized for bulk data insertion and briefly describe their advantages.
3. How does SQL Server handle XML data? Provide an example of how XML data can be queried or manipulated using T-SQL.
4. Define Dynamic SQL and outline its benefits and potential drawbacks. Provide an example scenario where Dynamic SQL would be advantageous.
5. What are Cursors in SQL Server? Explain when to use Cursors and their potential impact on database performance.

Exercise 6 – Long answer

1. Explain the significance of T-SQL in managing and manipulating data within SQL Server. Provide examples of commonly used T-SQL commands and their applications.

2. Describe the advantages and best practices of performing bulk operations in SQL Server. Discuss scenarios where bulk operations are beneficial and potential considerations.
3. Detail the functionalities and capabilities of working with XML data in SQL Server. Discuss how XML data can be stored, queried, and manipulated within the database.
4. Explain the concept of Dynamic SQL and its use cases in SQL Server. Provide examples demonstrating the construction and execution of Dynamic SQL queries.
5. Discuss the role of cursors in SQL Server and their impact on database performance. Provide examples illustrating the use of cursors and alternatives to mitigate performance issues.

Answer

Exercise 1:
Answer: 1: b, 2: a, 3: b, 4: c, 5: c, 6: a, 7: b, 8: b, 9: c, 10: b
Exercise 2:
Answer: 1: True, 2: True, 3: True, 4: True, 5: False, 6: False, 7: False, 8: False, 9: True, 10: True
Exercise 3:
Answer: 1: SELECT, INSERT, UPDATE, DELETE,2: BULK INSERT, BCP (Bulk Copy Program), 3: FOR XML, 4: programmatically, iterate, 5: DELETE, 6: BULK INSERT, 7: OPENXML, 8: Dynamic SQL, 9: INSERT, 10: BCP (Bulk Copy Program)
Exercise 4:
Answer: 1: Transact-SQL,2: BCP (Bulk Copy Program), 3: XML, 4: Dynamic SQL, 5: UPDATE, 6: Importing bulk data into a SQL Server table, 7: Generating XML output from SQL queries, 8: A database object used to retrieve and manipulate data row by row, 9: Removing records from a table, 10: OPENROWSET.

ONLINE RESOURCES

Practice Paper
Link: https://forms.office.com/r/zGiN4TmTtw?origin=lprLink
QR Code:

Chapter 8: Advanced Querying and Optimization

8.1 Query Optimization Techniques

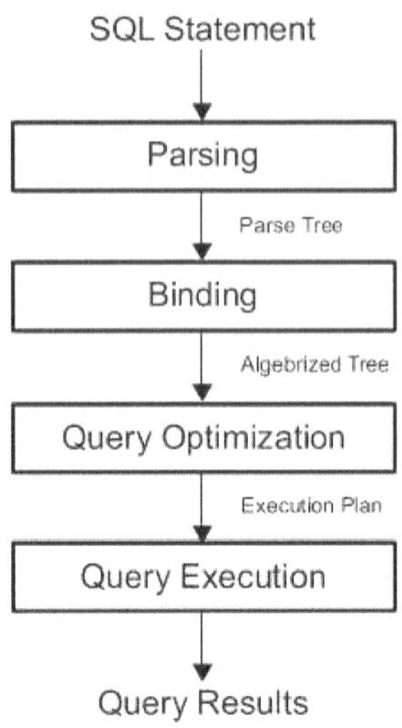

Optimizing queries in Microsoft SQL Server is crucial for enhancing database performance. Here are some query optimization techniques:

Indexing: Explain the significance of indexes in SQL Server. Discuss different types of indexes, their usage scenarios, and their impact on query performance. Provide examples of when to use clustered, non-clustered, and covering indexes.

Query Execution Plans: Detail the importance of query execution plans in optimizing queries. Discuss how to analyze and interpret execution plans using SQL Server tools. Provide examples of optimizing queries based on execution plan analysis.

Statistics and Data Distribution: Explain the role of statistics in query optimization. Discuss how SQL Server uses statistics to generate optimal query execution plans. Provide examples of updating statistics and how it affects query performance.

Query Rewriting and Refactoring: Discuss techniques for rewriting or refactoring queries to improve performance. Explain methods like subquery elimination, avoiding cursors, and using set-based operations.

Parameterization and Plan Reuse: Explain the importance of parameterization in SQL Server and how it impacts query plan reuse. Discuss techniques to encourage plan reuse and avoid unnecessary recompilations.

Table Partitioning: Describe table partitioning as a technique to improve query performance. Discuss how to implement table partitioning in SQL Server and its impact on query optimization.

Index Maintenance: Detail strategies for maintaining indexes to ensure optimal performance. Discuss how index fragmentation affects query performance and techniques for index maintenance.

Query Hints and Plan Forcing: Discuss the use of query hints to force specific query plans. Explain scenarios where query hints are beneficial and potential pitfalls.

Resource Governor and Query Prioritization: Explain the role of Resource Governor in SQL Server and how it can be used to prioritize certain queries or limit resources for specific workloads.

Monitoring and Profiling: Discuss the importance of monitoring and profiling tools in identifying performance bottlenecks. Explain how tools like SQL Server Profiler or Extended Events can be used for query optimization.

8.2 Performance Monitoring and Tuning

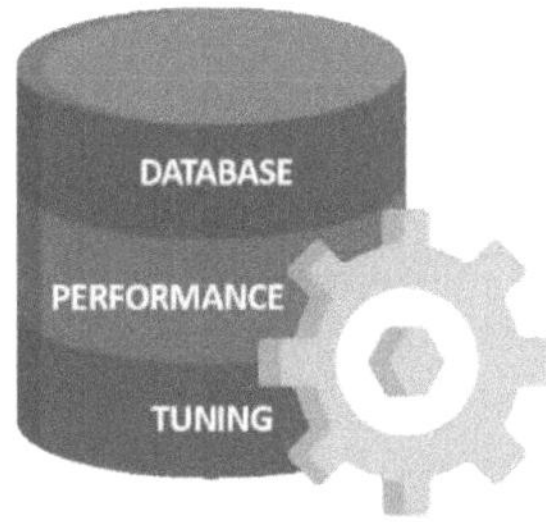

Performance monitoring and tuning in Microsoft SQL Server involves various aspects to enhance database efficiency. Here's an overview with examples:

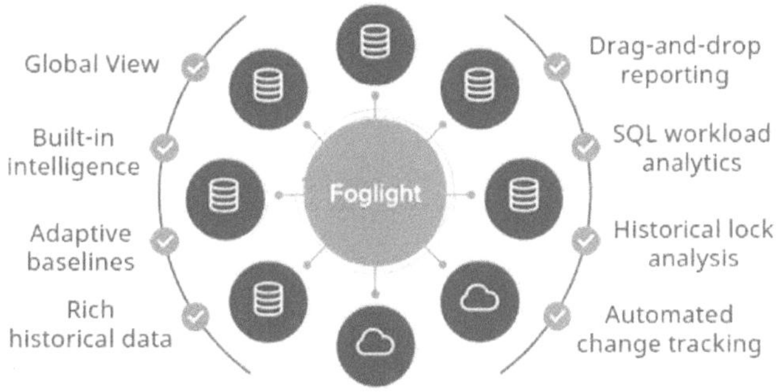

Index Optimization: Explain the significance of indexes in SQL Server performance. Discuss scenarios where certain types of indexes (clustered, non-clustered) are more suitable. Provide examples of optimizing queries by creating or altering indexes.

Example: Analyze a slow-performing query involving multiple joins and suggest appropriate indexes to improve its execution time. Explain the process of implementing these indexes and measure the performance impact.

Query Optimization: Describe query optimization techniques such as using execution plans, query hints, and re-writing queries to enhance performance. Discuss scenarios where restructuring a query or avoiding certain operations can significantly improve performance.

Example: Take a complex query and analyze its execution plan. Identify potential bottlenecks or inefficient operations and propose optimizations like restructuring joins, eliminating unnecessary columns, or using appropriate indexes.

Resource Management: Discuss the importance of resource allocation, memory management, and disk I/O in SQL Server performance. Explain how configuring memory settings, optimizing buffer pool, and managing disk space impact database performance.

Example: Demonstrate the impact of adjusting memory allocation settings on query execution time. Compare query performance before and after altering memory-related configurations.

Statistics and Maintenance: Explain the role of statistics in query optimization and database performance. Discuss maintenance tasks like updating statistics, index defragmentation, and database consistency checks to ensure optimal performance.

Example: Showcase the effect of outdated statistics on query plans and performance degradation. Perform maintenance tasks like updating statistics and measure the improvement in query execution.

Monitoring and Diagnostics: Describe monitoring tools, performance counters, and diagnostic techniques available in SQL Server for identifying performance issues. Explain how to use tools like SQL Server Profiler, Extended Events, or DMVs (Dynamic Management Views) for performance monitoring.

Example: Utilize SQL Server Profiler to capture and analyze a query's execution events, identify performance bottlenecks, and suggest strategies to address those issues.

Performance monitoring and tuning in SQL Server involve a mix of strategies focusing on query optimization, resource management, maintenance, and thorough monitoring to ensure efficient database operations.

8.3 Common Performance Issues and Solutions

performance issues in Microsoft SQL Server along with their potential solutions:

Query Performance: Queries running slow due to inadequate indexing, suboptimal query plans, or inefficient joins.

Solution: Review and optimize queries, add appropriate indexes, update statistics, and use tools like Execution Plans to identify bottlenecks.

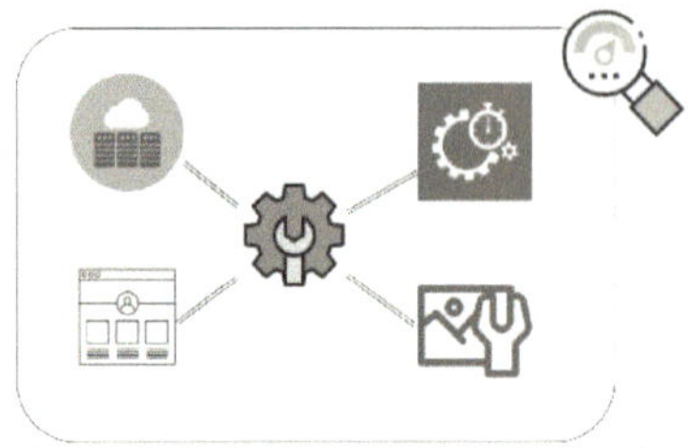

Locking and Blocking: Concurrent transactions causing contention, leading to blocking and performance degradation.

Solution: Adjust isolation levels, minimize transaction durations, use row-level locking, and optimize queries to reduce locking conflicts.

Insufficient Memory Allocation: SQL Server running out of memory, resulting in increased disk I/O and degraded performance.

Solution: Configure memory settings appropriately, utilize Buffer Pool Extension (BPE), and consider upgrading hardware for more RAM.

Fragmentation: Index and disk fragmentation impacting query performance and disk I/O operations.

Solution: Regularly defragment indexes, rebuild/reorganize fragmented indexes, and manage filegroups to reduce fragmentation.

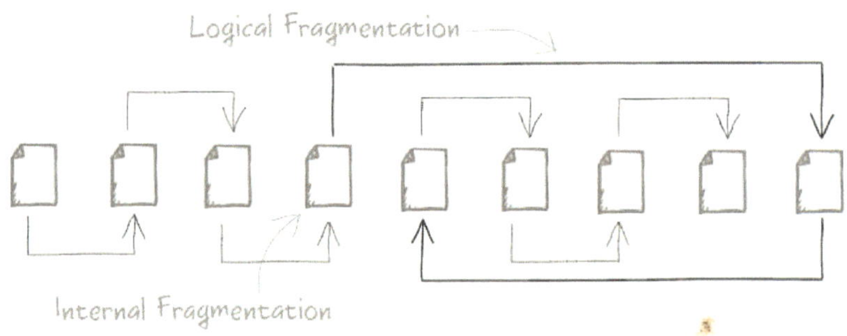

Hardware Limitations: Inadequate hardware resources affecting SQL Server performance.

Solution: Upgrade hardware components such as CPU, memory, and disk I/O subsystems to meet the server's demands.

I/O Bottlenecks: Disk subsystems becoming bottlenecks due to high read/write activity.

Solution: Distribute databases across multiple disks, use faster storage solutions (e.g., SSDs), and optimize I/O patterns to reduce contention.

TempDB Performance: TempDB contention causing slowdowns in multi-user environments.

Solution: Configure multiple TempDB data files, monitor TempDB usage, and optimize TempDB-related queries and operations.

Outdated Statistics: Inaccurate statistics leading to inefficient query plans.

Solution: Regularly update statistics on tables and indexes to ensure the query optimizer generates optimal execution plans.

Inefficient Database Design: Poorly designed databases impacting overall performance.

Solution: Normalize database structures, remove unnecessary indexes/columns, and optimize schema design to enhance performance.

Inadequate Maintenance: Lack of regular maintenance tasks impacting SQL Server's performance.

Solution: Implement routine maintenance plans for tasks like index rebuilds, integrity checks, and backups to ensure optimal performance.

By addressing these common performance issues through appropriate solutions and optimizations, SQL Server performance can be significantly improved, ensuring better responsiveness and stability.

8.4 Exercise

Exercise 1 – MCQ

1. Which of the following is an effective way to optimize query performance in SQL Server?

A) Increasing transaction duration

B) Using inefficient indexing

C) Utilizing proper indexing strategies

D) Avoiding parameterization
2. What tool can be used to analyze query execution plans in SQL Server for performance tuning?
A) SQL Profiler
B) Database Engine Tuning Advisor
C) Index Tuning Wizard
D) SQL Server Management Studio (SSMS)
3. To address locking and blocking in SQL Server, which technique can help minimize contention?
A) Decreasing transaction duration
B) Increasing isolation levels
C) Using a single TempDB data file
D) Reducing query optimization
4. What is the purpose of query hints in SQL Server?
A) To enforce query timeouts
B) To guide the query optimizer in generating efficient execution plans
C) To avoid using indexes
D) To force table scans
5. Which DMV (Dynamic Management View) provides information about index usage and missing indexes in SQL Server?
A) sys.dm_db_missing_index_details
B) sys.dm_os_wait_stats
C) sys.dm_exec_query_stats
D) sys.dm_db_index_usage_stats
6. What can be a potential solution for reducing I/O bottlenecks in SQL Server?
A) Using row-level locking
B) Increasing memory allocation
C) Using unclustered indexes
D) Using smaller TempDB data files
7. Which SQL statement is used to force an index to be used for a specific query in SQL Server?
A) USE INDEX
B) HINT INDEX
C) INDEX HINT
D) INDEX SEEK
8. What does the SQL Profiler tool in SQL Server allow DBAs to do?
A) Analyze execution plans
B) Monitor server activity and capture events
C) Generate missing index suggestions
D) Analyze database consistency checks
9. Which maintenance task can help reduce fragmentation in SQL Server?
A) CHECKTABLE
B) REBUILD INDEX
C) UPDATE STATISTICS
D) SHRINKDATABASE
10. Which SQL statement is used to limit the number of rows returned in a query result in SQL Server?
A) LIMIT
B) FETCH
C) TOP
D) OFFSET

Exercise 2 – True/ False

1. A clustered index is always faster for query performance compared to a non-clustered index.
2. SQL Profiler is primarily used for monitoring hardware performance metrics in SQL Server.
3. Using NOLOCK hint in SQL queries guarantees data consistency but can lead to dirty reads.
4. Scalar functions in SQL Server can impact query performance negatively, especially in large datasets.
5. Using the Database Engine Tuning Advisor (DTA) can automate query performance tuning in SQL Server.
6. Fragmentation primarily affects only non-clustered indexes, not clustered indexes.
7. Covering indexes are those that cover all columns in a table for faster query performance.

8. Buffer cache hit ratio is an accurate metric to measure overall SQL Server performance.
9. Increasing the number of TempDB data files can significantly improve performance in multi-core environments.
10. Using table variables always performs better than temporary tables due to lower overhead.

Exercise 3 – Fill in the blanks

1. The process of rearranging or structuring queries to improve _______________.
2. Regularly assessing database metrics to identify _______________ and applying changes for better performance.
3. A common solution for reducing locking conflicts is to adjust _______________.
4. The aim of query optimization is to generate _______________.
5. An important aspect of performance monitoring is analyzing _______________ to pinpoint areas for improvement.
6. Insufficient _______________ can lead to SQL Server running out of memory.
7. _______________ assist in reducing the time taken for query execution by storing frequently used data.
8. Utilizing _______________ tools helps in identifying bottlenecks and resource-intensive queries.
9. _______________ help minimize fragmentation and optimize disk I/O operations.
10. Reducing unnecessary _______________ or join operations can optimize query performance.

Exercise 4 – One word answer

1. What is the primary objective of optimizing queries?
2. What tool helps visualize query execution paths?
3. What does defragmentation aim to reduce in indexes?
4. What describes the individual operations in an execution plan?
5. What does BPE stand for in SQL Server memory optimization?
6. What can lead to blocking in concurrent transactions?
7. What aims to reduce redundancy in a database?
8. What is the recommended number of TempDB data files for multi-core CPUs?
9. What maintenance task enhances query optimization?
10. What can improve SQL Server performance if lacking?

Exercise 5 – Small answer

1. Define "Query Plan" in SQL Server optimization. How does it impact query performance?
2. Briefly explain the role of "Index Fragmentation" in SQL Server performance. How can you address this issue?
3. What is "Blocking" in SQL Server and how does it impact database performance? Suggest one method to mitigate blocking.
4. Name one technique to optimize queries by reducing the amount of data transferred between the SQL Server and the client application.
5. How does "Query Statistics" help in performance tuning? Name one SQL Server tool used to gather query statistics.

Exercise 6 – Long answer

1. Describe the significance of query optimization in database management systems. Illustrate at least three query optimization techniques used to enhance SQL query performance. Provide a detailed explanation of how each technique contributes to improving query execution efficiency.
2. Explain the key steps involved in performance monitoring and tuning for a database system. Elaborate on the role of query execution plans and statistics in performance monitoring. Discuss how indexing and schema design impact performance tuning strategies.
3. Identify three common performance issues encountered in database systems. For each issue, provide a detailed description of its causes and potential impact on system performance. Offer specific strategies or solutions to mitigate these issues, highlighting the steps involved in implementing these solutions.
4. Discuss the challenges associated with optimizing queries for large datasets. Explain how techniques like partitioning, data denormalization, and indexing are utilized to enhance query performance for extensive databases. Provide real-world examples showcasing the effectiveness of these techniques.
5. Define the concept of a query execution plan and its significance in optimizing SQL queries. Describe the components of a query execution plan and explain how analyzing this plan helps in identifying bottlenecks and improving query performance. Provide a step-by-step guide on interpreting and analyzing a query execution plan using relevant examples.

Answer

Exercise 1:
Answer: 1: C, 2: D, 3: B, 4: B, 5: A, 6: B, 7: A, 8: B, 9: B, 10: C
Exercise 2:
Answer: 1: False, 2: False, 3: True, 4: True, 5: True, 6: False 7: False, 8: False, 9: True, 10: False
Exercise 3:
Answer: 1: performance or execution efficiency,2: performance bottlenecks or inefficiencies, 3: isolation levels, 4: optimal or efficient execution plans, 5: execution plans or query plans, 6: memory allocation or inadequate memory, 7: Caching mechanisms or query caches, 8: profiling or monitoring, 9: Index maintenance or defragmentation tasks, 10: table scans or unnecessary reads.
Exercise 4:
Answer: 1: Performance, 2: Profiler, 3: Fragmentation, 4: Operators, 5: Extension, 6: Contention, 7: Normalization, 8: Cores, 9: Statistics, 10: Hardware.

ONLINE RESOURCES

Practice Paper
Link: https://forms.office.com/r/HSDAUCU2bH?origin=lprLink
QR Code:

Chapter 9: High Availability and Disaster Recovery

9.1 Backup and Restore Strategies

Backup Strategies:

Full Backup:

Description: Captures the entire database, including data, schema, indexes, and system tables.

Usage: It serves as a baseline for other backups like differential and transaction log backups.

Differential Backup:

Description: Stores changes made since the last full backup, reducing the backup duration compared to full backups.

Usage: Useful for frequent backups; however, the size depends on the volume of changes made.

Transaction Log Backup:

Description: Captures transaction log changes to ensure point-in-time recovery.

Usage: Enables recovery to a specific point in time in case of a disaster or data loss.

File and Filegroup Backup:

Description: Backs up specific files or filegroups within a database rather than the entire database.

Usage: Provides flexibility in restoring specific portions of a database.

Copy-only Backup:

Description: Allows for an ad-hoc backup without disrupting the regular backup sequence.

Usage: Useful when a backup is needed outside of the regular backup schedule.

Snapshot Backup:

Description: Utilizes storage snapshots to create backups instantly without impacting the source database.

Usage: Provides an instantaneous and low-impact backup method.

Example: This depends on the storage system and its integration with SQL Server, often managed externally.

Restore Strategies:

Full Database Restore:

Description: This method involves restoring the entire database from a previously created full backup.

Process: Using a full backup file, typically created as a baseline, the entire database is restored to the state captured at the time of the full backup.

Use Case: Primarily used for complete recovery after a catastrophic failure or when moving databases between servers.

Point-in-Time Recovery:

Description: Utilizes both full and transaction log backups to restore the database to a specific point in time.

Process: Combines full backups with subsequent transaction log backups, allowing restoration to a specific moment in the past.

Use Case: Useful when reverting to a specific state or time before data corruption or erroneous changes occurred.

File and Filegroup Restore:

Description: Offers the ability to restore specific files or filegroups rather than the entire database.

Process: Allows for restoring data in a more granular fashion, which can be beneficial in scenarios where only a portion of the database is affected or requires recovery.

Use Case: Often used for restoring specific filegroups or damaged files without affecting the entire database.

Page-Level Restore:

Description: Enables the restoration of individual damaged pages within a database.

Process: Allows for pinpointing and restoring only the specific pages that are corrupt or damaged, avoiding the need for a full database restore.

Use Case: Useful in situations where only a few pages are corrupted, limiting the impact on the entire database.

Online Restore:

Description: Conducts restoration operations while the database remains online and accessible for users.

Process: Allows for continuous database availability during the restoration process, reducing downtime and ensuring access to critical data.

Use Case: Suitable for environments that require 24/7 accessibility and cannot afford prolonged downtimes.

Piecemeal Restore:

Description: Focuses on restoring crucial components or filegroups of the database to bring them online quickly.

Process: Enables the restoration of essential parts of the database to a functional state without restoring the entire database.

Use Case: Helps in scenarios where only specific critical components need to be available promptly, reducing downtime for those components.

Examples:

Full Backup:

```
BACKUP DATABASE [DatabaseName] TO DISK = 'D:\Backup\DatabaseName_Full.bak' WITH INIT
```

Transaction Log Backup:

```
BACKUP LOG [DatabaseName] TO DISK = 'D:\Backup\DatabaseName_Log.trn' WITH INIT
```

Full Database Restore:

```
USE master
RESTORE DATABASE [RestoredDatabase] FROM DISK = 'D:\Backup\DatabaseName_Full.bak' WITH REPLACE
```

Point-in-Time Recovery:

```
RESTORE DATABASE [DatabaseName] FROM DISK = 'D:\Backup\DatabaseName_Full.bak'
WITH NORECOVERY;

RESTORE LOG [DatabaseName] FROM DISK = 'D:\Backup\DatabaseName_Log.trn'
WITH STOPAT = '2023-11-16 12:00:00', RECOVERY;
```

These strategies help ensure data availability, integrity, and recovery capabilities in the event of system failures or data loss.

9.2 Log Shipping and Mirroring

Log Shipping in Microsoft SQL Server:

Log shipping is a disaster recovery technique where transaction log backups from a primary database are automatically applied to a secondary database. This secondary database can be used for reporting or disaster recovery purposes.

Example:

Setup Primary Database:

Configure the primary database for log backups.

Set up a job to take regular transaction log backups (e.g., every 15 minutes).

Secondary Database Configuration:

Restore a full backup of the primary database on the secondary server.

Configure log shipping by setting up jobs to copy transaction log backups from the primary server to the secondary server and restore them.

Monitoring and Failover:

Monitor log shipping jobs to ensure backups are copied and applied on the secondary database without issues.

In case of a disaster on the primary server, initiate a failover by manually bringing the secondary database online.

Database Mirroring in Microsoft SQL Server:

Database mirroring is a high-availability solution that creates and maintains a standby copy of a database. It operates in two modes: high-safety (synchronous) and high-performance (asynchronous).

Example:

Setting up Mirroring:

Configure a principal database and a mirror database.

Establish a mirroring session between the principal and mirror servers.

Operating Modes:

High-Safety Mode: Transactions are committed on the principal and then synchronized with the mirror to ensure data consistency.

High-Performance Mode: Transactions are committed on the principal without waiting for the mirror to commit, leading to potential data loss in case of failure.

Monitoring and Failover:

Monitor the mirroring status to ensure synchronization and detect potential issues.

In case of a principal server failure, manually initiate a failover to the mirror server to continue operations.

Both log shipping and database mirroring are used for fault tolerance and disaster recovery, but they differ in their implementation, failover mechanisms, and the level of data protection they provide.

9.3 Clustering and Always on Availability Groups

Clustering in Microsoft SQL Server refers to the technique of creating a clustered index on a table. This index sorts and stores the table's rows based on the key values and dictates the physical order of data in the table. Here's an example to illustrate clustering:

Example:

Consider a table named **EmployeeDetails** with columns: **EmployeeID**, **FirstName**, **LastName**, **Department**, and **Salary**.

```
-- Creating a table
CREATE TABLE EmployeeDetails (
    EmployeeID INT PRIMARY KEY,
    FirstName NVARCHAR(50),
    LastName NVARCHAR(50),
    Department NVARCHAR(50),
    Salary DECIMAL(10, 2)
);

-- Adding data to the table
INSERT INTO EmployeeDetails VALUES
(1, 'Ram', 'SHarma', 'IT', 60000.00),
(2, 'Rahul', 'Verma', 'HR', 55000.00),
(3, 'Anjali', 'Sharma', 'Finance', 65000.00),
(4, 'Karan', 'Patel', 'IT', 62000.00),
(5, 'Neha', 'Shrivastava', 'HR', 58000.00);
```

Clustering Example:

Let's create a clustered index on the **EmployeeID** column:

```
-- Creating a clustered index
CREATE CLUSTERED INDEX IX_EmployeeID ON EmployeeDetails(EmployeeID);
```

Now, the **EmployeeDetails** table is clustered based on the **EmployeeID** column. This means the physical order of rows in the table matches the order of the **EmployeeID**. When querying data based on **EmployeeID**, SQL Server can directly access the corresponding rows quickly because they are physically stored in the same order as the index.

Benefits of Clustering:

Faster retrieval of data based on the clustered key.

Improved performance for range-based queries on the clustered key.

Reduces the need for sorting and improves query execution.

It's essential to choose the clustered index key wisely, as it directly affects the physical storage and retrieval of data in the table.

Always On Availability Groups (AGs) in Microsoft SQL Server provide high availability and disaster recovery solutions. Here's an overview with an example:

Overview:

Always On Availability Groups is a feature that enables high availability and disaster recovery solutions at the database level. It allows you to create groups of user databases that fail over together. These groups are known as availability groups.

Example:

Let's consider a scenario of an e-commerce platform using SQL Server. The platform has critical databases for customer information, order details, and inventory.

Setting up Always On Availability Groups:

Prerequisites: Ensure that multiple SQL Server instances are set up and connected across different nodes or servers.

Creating Availability Groups: Create an availability group named "ECommerceAG" and add the critical databases related to customers, orders, and inventory.

Replica Configuration: Configure synchronous or asynchronous data replication between primary and secondary replicas for data redundancy.

Failover Testing: Simulate failover scenarios to test the failover process and ensure data integrity and accessibility during failover events.

Monitoring and Management: Regularly monitor the health of replicas, check synchronization status, and manage automatic failover settings.

Benefits:

High Availability: Minimize downtime by quickly switching to a secondary replica in case of primary database failure.

Disaster Recovery: Ensure data redundancy and disaster recovery capabilities across different servers or locations.

Readable Secondary Replicas: Use secondary replicas for read-only operations, offloading read workloads from the primary database.

Considerations:

Networking and Infrastructure: Ensure robust network connectivity between replicas to maintain data synchronization.

Licensing and Resources: Understand licensing requirements and allocate appropriate resources for multiple replicas.

Conclusion:

Always On Availability Groups provide a robust solution for ensuring high availability, disaster recovery, and improved scalability for critical databases in Microsoft SQL Server environments.

9.4 Failover and Data Replication

Failover in Microsoft SQL Server refers to the process of transitioning from a primary database server to a secondary or standby server when the primary server becomes unavailable. This is typically part of a high availability (HA) and disaster recovery (DR) strategy to ensure minimal downtime and data loss.

Failover Types:

High Availability (HA) Failover:

- **Automatic Failover:** Occurs when a primary server becomes inaccessible due to hardware or software issues, and the failover process automatically redirects clients to a secondary server.
- **Manual Failover:** Requires manual intervention to switch from the primary server to the secondary server.

Disaster Recovery (DR) Failover:

- **Planned Failover:** Used during maintenance or upgrades when administrators want to switch the workload from one server to another intentionally.
- **Unplanned Failover:** Triggered by unexpected events like server failures, power outages, or natural disasters.

Failover Processes:

Mirroring Failover: Utilizes a principal and mirror server; when the principal fails, the mirror server takes over. Automatic and manual failovers are supported.

Always On Failover Cluster Instances (FCI): A Windows Server Failover Cluster (WSFC) configuration where SQL Server instances fail over between nodes in a cluster.

Always On Availability Groups (AG): A feature that enables a set of user databases to fail over together as a single unit. It provides automatic and manual failover options.

Failover Considerations:

Automatic vs. Manual: Depending on the configuration and requirements, failover can be automatic or require manual intervention.

Data Synchronization: Ensuring that data remains consistent between primary and secondary servers is crucial to minimize data loss during failover.

Failover Testing: Regularly testing failover scenarios helps identify potential issues and ensures the failover process works as expected during a real outage.

Failover in Detail:

Failover Process: Initiating a failover involves detecting the primary server's failure, promoting the secondary server to take over its role, and redirecting client connections to the new primary server.
Failover Detection: Monitoring mechanisms constantly check the primary server's health. If it becomes unresponsive or experiences issues beyond a threshold, failover triggers.
Client Redirection: After a successful failover, clients need to be directed to the new primary server to resume operations seamlessly.
Failover Benefits:
High Availability: Ensures minimal downtime, allowing applications to remain accessible even during server failures.
Business Continuity: Provides a robust disaster recovery strategy to safeguard critical data and operations.
Improved Reliability: Reduces the impact of potential server failures on ongoing operations.
Microsoft SQL Server offers various failover solutions catering to different deployment scenarios, ensuring business continuity and minimal disruptions in case of server failures.
Data replication in Microsoft SQL Server refers to the process of duplicating and maintaining copies of data across multiple databases or servers. Here's an overview:
Data Replication:
Definition: Data replication involves copying data from one database to another to ensure consistency, availability, and reliability.
Purpose: Enables distribution of data for various purposes like scalability, availability, reporting, and disaster recovery.
Types of Replications:
- **Snapshot Replication**: Entire data snapshot is taken and applied to subscribers periodically.
- **Transactional Replication**: Captures and replicates changes as they occur, maintaining consistency among databases.
- **Merge Replication**: Enables changes in both the publisher and subscriber databases, merging updates periodically.

Components:
- **Publisher**: Database providing data to be replicated.
- **Distributor**: Manages the flow of data to subscribers.
- **Subscriber**: Database receiving replicated data.

Replication Agents: Processes responsible for replication tasks, such as the Snapshot Agent, Log Reader Agent, and Distribution Agent.
Implementation and Configuration:
Publication: Defines what data to replicate and how.
Subscription: Specifies the location and settings for replicated data.
Replication Types and Configuration:
- Setting up publications and subscriptions.
- Configuring replication schedules.
- Defining rules for conflict resolution (in merge replication).

Monitoring and Troubleshooting:
- Monitoring replication status using SQL Server Management Studio.
- Diagnosing and resolving replication conflicts or failures.

Advantages and Use Cases:
Advantages:
- Improved performance for distributed applications.
- Enhanced scalability and availability.
- Support for reporting and analytics on replicated data.

Use Cases:
- Geographically distributed applications requiring low latency.
- Load balancing across multiple servers.
- Disaster recovery and failover scenarios.

Best Practices and Considerations:
Maintenance:
- Regular monitoring of replication health.
- Maintenance of indexes and statistics to optimize performance.

Security:
- Securing communication channels between publisher, distributor, and subscribers.

Performance:

Considering network bandwidth for efficient data transfer.

Consistency:

Ensuring proper conflict resolution strategies.

Scalability and Disaster Recovery:

Planning for scalability and disaster recovery with replicated data.

Conclusion:

Data replication in SQL Server provides flexibility, scalability, and reliability in managing distributed data, catering to various business needs and scenarios. It's crucial to plan, configure, and maintain replication setups for optimal performance and data consistency.

9.5 Exercise

Exercise 1 – MCQ

1. Which strategy involves creating and storing duplicates of a database to ensure data restoration in case of system failure?
A) Log Shipping
B) Clustering
C) Backup and Restore
D) Data Replication

2. Which technique continuously sends transaction logs from one database to another in real-time for standby or reporting purposes?
A) Clustering
B) Log Shipping
C) Mirroring
D) Always on Availability Groups

3. What mechanism ensures high availability by using multiple servers to operate as a single system?
A) Failover
B) Data Replication
C) Clustering
D) Backup and Restore

4. In disaster recovery, what does the term RTO refer to?
A) Recovery Time Objective
B) Recovery Technique Outcome
C) Recovery Track Order
D) Recovered Total Operations

5. Which strategy involves creating multiple copies of a database and automatically failing over to another copy if one fails?
A) Data Replication
B) Log Shipping
C) Clustering
D) Always on Availability Groups

6. Which technique replicates changes in real-time from one database to another to maintain identical copies?
A) Clustering
B) Mirroring
C) Data Replication
D) Backup and Restore

7. What is the primary purpose of log shipping?
A) Automatic failover
B) Load balancing
C) Reporting
D) Disaster recovery

8. In clustering, what ensures high availability by allowing a secondary server to take over when the primary fails?
A) Failback
B) Failover
C) Mirroring
D) Log Shipping

9. Which SQL Server feature enables the grouping of multiple databases to failover together?
A) Always on Availability Groups
B) Clustering
C) Data Replication
D) Mirroring
10. What's the main objective of clustering in SQL Server?
A) Load balancing
B) High availability
C) Log shipping
D) Data replication

Exercise 2 – True/ False

1. Backups are only essential for production databases.
2. Log shipping and database mirroring offer the same level of failover capability.
3. Clustering provides higher scalability than Always On Availability Groups.
4. Data replication ensures immediate failover in case of server crashes.
5. Regular backups can be stored on the same disk as the production database.
6. Database mirroring requires more resources compared to log shipping.
7. Clustering allows the grouping of multiple physical servers to act as a single server.
8. Failover mechanisms are primarily used for planned maintenance purposes.
9. The recovery model does not affect the backup and restore strategy.
10. Log shipping is asynchronous, while database mirroring is synchronous.

Exercise 3 – Fill in the blanks

1. Regular __________ are essential for preserving data integrity and facilitating recovery in case of failures.
2. Log shipping involves transferring transaction logs from a primary database to one or more __________ databases.
3. Clustering enables the creation of a __________ environment, where multiple servers work together to provide high availability.
4. __________ is the process of switching over to a standby server when the primary server fails.
5. A __________ strategy helps ensure continuous availability and redundancy by replicating data across multiple locations.
6. For disaster recovery, it's crucial to have __________ in place to recover the database to a specific point in time.
7. Always on Availability Groups in SQL Server offer __________, providing an alternative to database mirroring.
8. __________ involves creating multiple copies of a database to prevent data loss in the event of a hardware failure.
9. __________ involves maintaining two or more copies of data in different geographic locations for fault tolerance.
10. During a __________, the system automatically switches to a secondary server to maintain service availability.

Exercise 4 – One word answer

1. What is a common strategy for safeguarding data against accidental loss?
2. What is the term for creating redundant copies of data in multiple locations for safety?
3. Which method is used to maintain a secondary database that is updated regularly with transactions from the primary database?
4. What's the technology ensuring continuous database availability by enabling automatic failover?
5. What's the process of duplicating an entire database for failover purposes?
6. Which feature provides a high availability solution by grouping databases?
7. What's the primary purpose of Log Shipping?
8. What's the term for the process of switching to a secondary server in case of a primary server failure?
9. What's the main benefit of clustering in database management?
10. What is the purpose of replication in database systems?

Exercise 5 – Small answer

1. Log shipping involves automatically sending transaction log backups from one database (primary) to a secondary database.
2. Availability Groups is a feature in SQL Server that allows you to define a group of user databases that fail over together.

3. Data replication involves copying data from one database to another to ensure redundancy and fault tolerance.
4. Clustering ensures continuous availability by grouping servers to maintain services and prevent system failure.
5. Log shipping allows you to maintain standby databases by continuously backing up transaction logs from a primary database.

Exercise 6 – Long answer

1. Elaborate on the concept of log shipping and database mirroring in Azure. Discuss their role in maintaining high availability and disaster recovery. Compare and contrast these methods, highlighting their strengths and limitations.
2. Define clustering and Always On Availability Groups in Azure. Explain how they contribute to ensuring high availability and fault tolerance in a database environment. Provide a step-by-step process for setting up these configurations.
3. Describe the benefits and challenges associated with implementing automated backup and recovery policies in Azure. Discuss best practices for configuring automated backups and restoring data in different Azure services.
4. Compare and contrast various high availability solutions offered by Azure, such as geo-replication, virtual machine scale sets, and Azure Site Recovery. Evaluate their suitability for different scenarios based on factors like cost, complexity, and recovery time objectives (RTOs).
5. Explore the cost implications of implementing high availability and disaster recovery solutions in Azure. Analyze the trade-offs between cost-effectiveness and ensuring maximum uptime.

Answer

Exercise 1:
Answer: 1: C, 2: B, 3: C, 4: A, 5: D, 6: C, 7: D, 8: B, 9: A, 10: B
Exercise 2:
Answer: 1: False, 2: False, 3: False, 4: True, 5: False, 6: True 7: True, 8: False, 9: False, 10: True
Exercise 3:
Answer: 1: backups,2: secondary, 3: clustered, 4: Failover, 5: replication, 6: backups, 7: high availability, 8: DATABASE, 9: mirroring, 10: failover.
Exercise 4:
Answer: 1: Backup, 2: Replication, 3: Log Shipping, 4: Clustering, 5: Mirroring, 6: Availability Groups, 7: Disaster Recovery, 8: Failover, 9: Fault Tolerance, 10: Redundancy.

ONLINE RESOURCES

Practice Paper
Link: https://forms.office.com/r/y24dN1yK91?origin=lprLink
QR Code:

Chapter 10: Security and Permissions

10.1 Authentication Modes

In Microsoft SQL Server, authentication modes determine how users connect to the database. There are two primary authentication modes:

Windows Authentication (Integrated Security):

Description: Relies on Windows user accounts to authenticate users. Users connect to SQL Server using their Windows credentials, removing the need to provide a separate username and password.

Example: A user logs into their Windows account and then accesses SQL Server using Windows Authentication. SQL Server verifies the user's Windows credentials.

SQL Server Authentication:

Description: Requires users to provide a username and password explicitly to access SQL Server.

Example: A user provides a SQL Server username and password when connecting to the SQL Server instance. SQL Server verifies these credentials against its internal database.

Permissions in SQL Server control access to objects within the database. These permissions can be granted to users or roles to perform specific actions. Examples include:

GRANT: Allows users or roles to perform specific actions or operations within the database, such as SELECT, INSERT, UPDATE, DELETE, etc.

DENY: Explicitly denies a user or role permission to perform an action, even if it's granted elsewhere.

REVOKE: Removes previously granted permissions from a user or role.

For instance, consider a scenario where a user 'UserA' wants to access a table 'SalesData'. Using SQL Server Management Studio (SSMS), an administrator can grant SELECT permission to 'UserA' on the 'SalesData' table. This allows 'UserA' to retrieve data from the 'SalesData' table but restricts other operations like DELETE or UPDATE unless explicitly granted.

Additionally, SQL Server allows the creation of roles to group users and manage permissions efficiently. For example, an 'Admin' role might have full access to multiple tables, while a 'ReadOnly' role might only have SELECT permissions.

SQL Server - Windows Authentication

SQL Server supports the two layers of authentication: login and database user. Login is the first layer of security to access and connect to the SQL Server. A login has nothing to do with the databases. Instead, login is mapped to a user in a database to read or write to a particular database.

There are two authentication modes in SQL Server using which you can login and connect with the SQL Server.

Windows Authentication

SQL Server Authentication

Windows Authentication

Windows authentication mode enables local Windows authentication with SQL Server, where you can login with your local Windows credentials.

For example, the following uses a Windows credential to connect to SQL Server where user in MYDBSERVER\user is the local user account on Windows and MYDBSERVER is the name of the database server. Click OK to login with this credentials and connect to the MYDBSERVER database server.

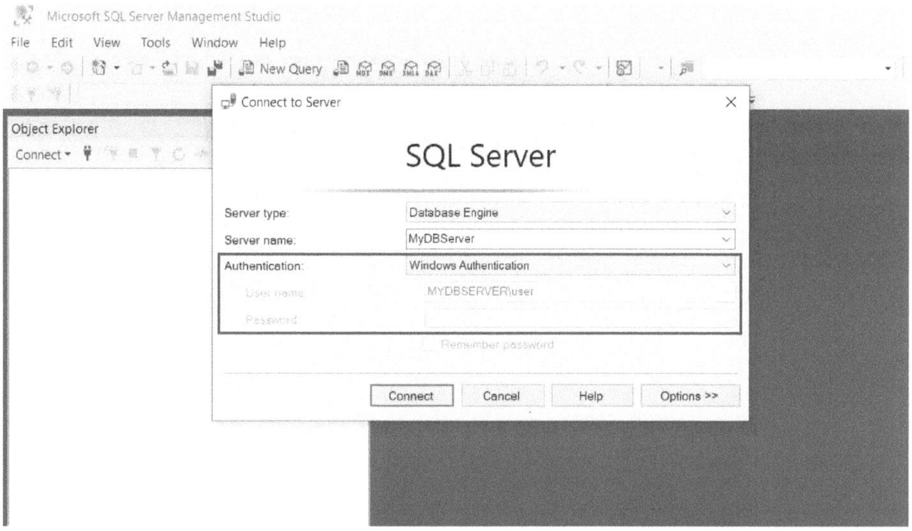

Windows authentication is the default authentication mode and is more secure than SQL Server authentication. It is also referred to as integrated security which is tightly integrated with Windows. Users who are already authenticated with Windows and need not provide any additional credentials while connecting to SQL Server. It is also called a trusted connection. The user account is confirmed by Windows.

In Windows authentication, login can be created in SQL Server for an entire Windows group which simplifies managing account administration.

Windows authentication uses Kerberos security protocol, provides password policy enforcement, and supports password expiration.

Let's see how to create a new login that uses local Window's user account to connect with the SQL Server.

Create a New Login with Windows Authentication

To create a new login, open SQL Server Management Studio.

In the object explorer, expand the **Security** folder and right-click on the Logins folder and click **New Login...**, as shown below.

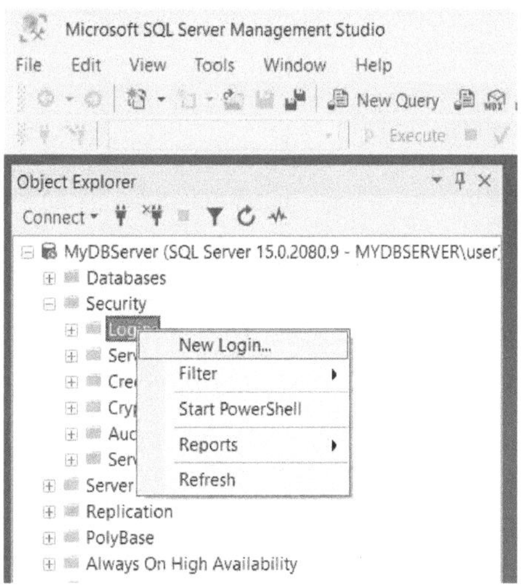

In the Login –New window, shown below, enter a Windows user name. If a user name is not a Windows user then it will raise an error. You may click on the Search button to search a Windows user, as shown below.

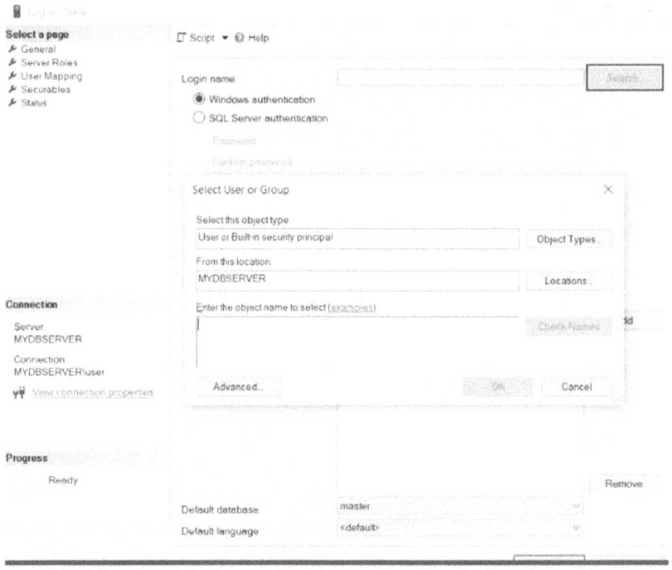

After entering a login name, you will have to choose either Windows authentication or SQL Server authentication. Select Windows authentication. Notice that the password field and password policy radio buttons will be disabled for Windows authentication because we will use the Windows credentials here.

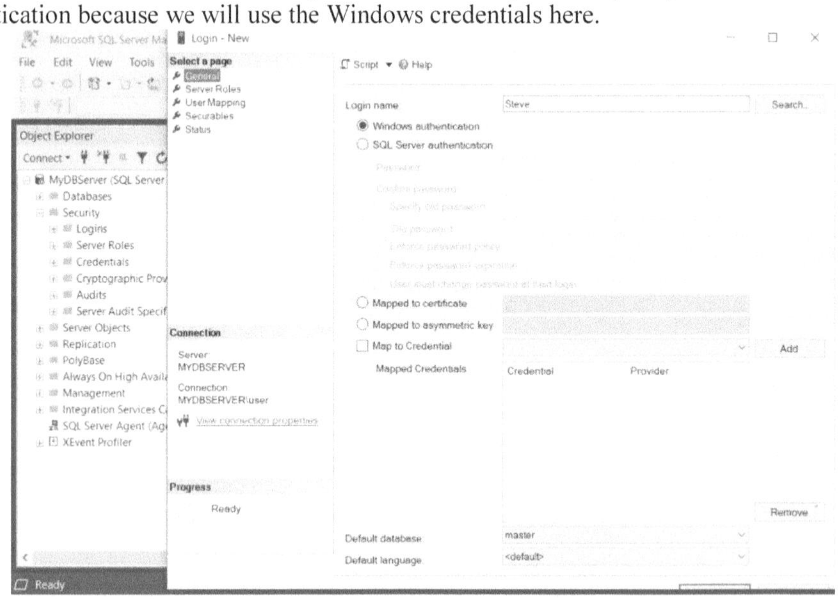

Now, to assign roles & permission to the new login, go to the Server Roles tab. On the Server Roles page, you can assign the server-level role to the new login by clicking the checkbox next to the role. By default, the public role is assigned to a new login. Additionally, let us assign the sysadmin role by clicking on the checkbox next to sysadmin. With sysadmin server role, user can perform any activity on the server and has full control.

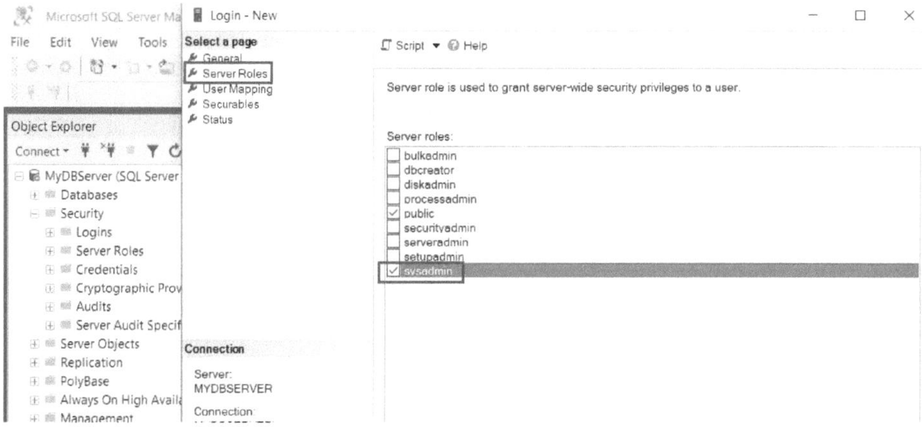

Click the User mapping tab. Here, we will map our Windows login to a database user.

It lists all the databases on the server. To map your new login, just select checkboxes next to databases for which you want map this login to access a database.

In the below figure **AdventureWorks2019** database is selected. The new login is now listed under the User column for AdventureWorks2019. You can change the user name if you want it to give a different name than your login name. Just click on the name and re-type whichever name you want for the user. If you want more databases associated with your login, then just click the checkbox next to the database, and it will be mapped with the login.

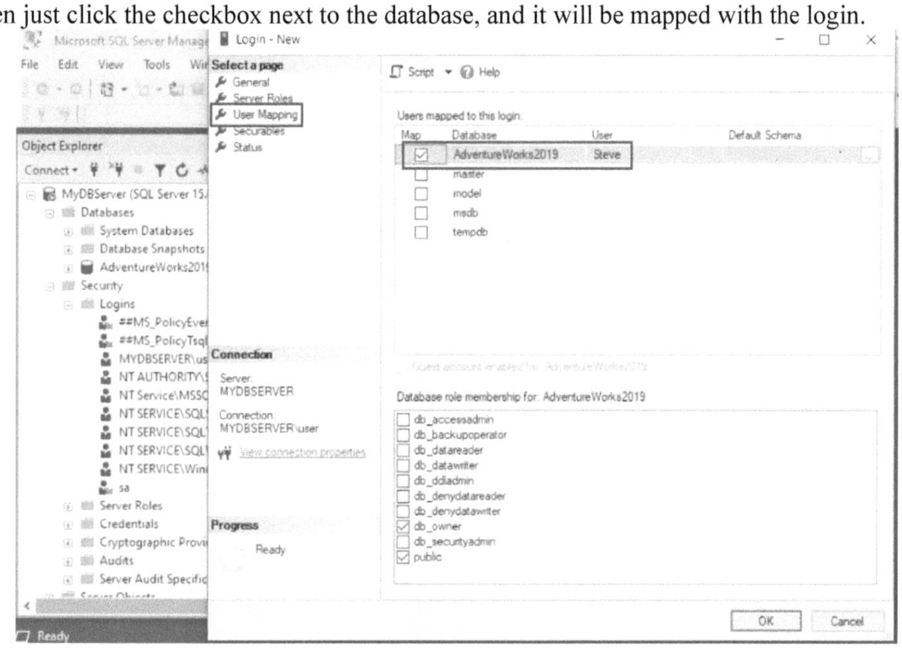

Now, click on the Securables tab. Securables are SQL server resources that can be accessed by a login you are creating. On the Securables tab, click on the Search button. This will open a pop-up, as shown below. Select The server '<Your Server name>' and click OK. This will list all the explicit permissions for a server. Select Grant, With Grant, or Deny as per your requirement.

This is an optional step. You may skip Securables settings while creating the login, and set it later.

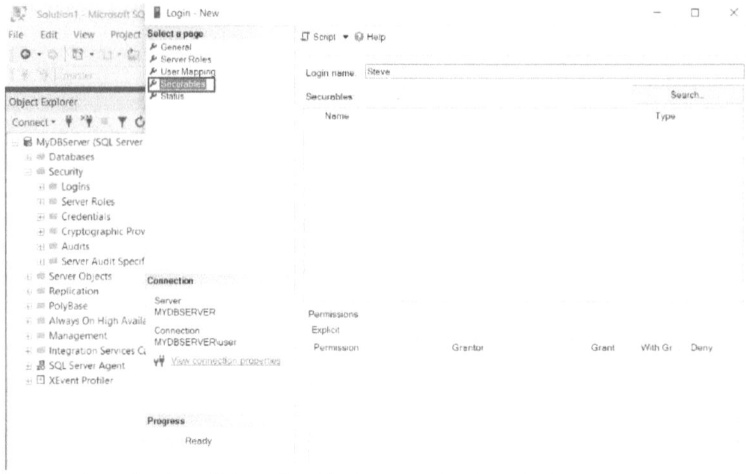

Finally, click on the Status tab and select "Grant" radio button for Permission to connect to the database engine, and Enabled radio button for Login, as shown below.

Click Ok to create the new login. This will add a new login under the Logins node.

10.2 Authorization and Permissions

In Microsoft SQL Server, authorization and permissions are crucial for controlling access to databases, objects within databases, and server-level resources. Here's an overview:

Authorization Concepts:

Principals:

Principals in SQL Server are entities that request or access resources within the database. They include:

Logins: Credentials used for authentication to the SQL Server instance.

Users: Mapped to logins and associated with specific databases. Users are the ones who execute queries, perform actions, and interact with database objects.

Roles: A group of permissions that can be assigned to multiple users. Roles can simplify security management by granting sets of permissions collectively.

Applications: Represented by application roles or specific permissions for an application's service account.

Securables:

Securables are the objects within the database that can have permissions assigned to them. Some common securables include:

Tables: The fundamental storage unit in a relational database, containing rows and columns.

Views: Virtual tables that display the results of a stored query.

Stored Procedures: Precompiled collections of SQL statements stored within the database.

Functions: User-defined or system functions that perform operations on data.

Schemas: Logical containers for database objects, often used for better organization.

Assemblies: Objects used to store compiled code (e.g., .NET assemblies).

Permissions:

Permissions in SQL Server define rules that control what actions can be performed on securables. Permissions are granted to principals and enable them to perform specific operations on the securables. Common permissions include:
SELECT: Allows reading data from a table or view.
INSERT: Permits adding new rows of data into a table.
UPDATE: Enables modifying existing data in a table.
DELETE: Allows removing rows from a table.
EXECUTE: Grants the ability to execute stored procedures or functions.
CONTROL: Provides complete control over a securable.

Applying Permissions:

Permissions are applied using the GRANT, DENY, and REVOKE statements:
GRANT: Assigns permissions to a user or role. For instance, GRANT SELECT ON [Table] TO [User].
DENY: Explicitly denies a specific permission, even if it was granted earlier.
REVOKE: Removes previously granted permissions, e.g., REVOKE SELECT ON [Table] FROM [User].

Permission Hierarchy:

Server-Level Permissions:

Server-level permissions are the highest level of access control in SQL Server, governing actions at the server instance level. These permissions include:
Creating Databases: Ability to create new databases within the server instance.
Altering Server Settings: Permissions to configure server-wide settings, such as memory allocation, security configurations, and other server-level parameters.
Creating Logins and Users: Rights to create logins and users that can access the server.
Configuring Server Properties: Permission to change server properties like collation, default language, etc.
Server-level permissions are granted to server-level principals such as logins or server roles. These permissions apply across all databases hosted by the SQL Server instance.

Database-Level Permissions:

Database-level permissions control actions within a specific database. They are assigned to users or roles and include:
Access to Objects: Permissions for CRUD operations (CREATE, READ, UPDATE, DELETE) on tables, views, stored procedures, etc.
Schema-Level Permissions: Control over schemas within the database, such as creating, altering, or dropping schemas.
Backup and Restore: Authorization to perform database backup and restore operations.
Granting Other Permissions: Ability to grant permissions to other users or roles within the same database.
Database-level permissions are more granular and focused on actions that directly affect the data and objects within a specific database.

Object-Level Permissions:

Object-level permissions define access rights to specific database objects like tables, views, stored procedures, or functions. Examples include:
SELECT Permission: Grants the ability to read data from a table or view.
INSERT Permission: Allows adding new records to a table.
UPDATE Permission: Permits modification of existing data in a table.
DELETE Permission: Authorizes the deletion of records from a table.
These permissions are assigned directly to users or roles and regulate the operations users can perform on individual database objects.

Granting and Managing Permissions:

Permissions are managed using SQL commands like GRANT, DENY, and REVOKE. These commands allow DBAs to assign, restrict, or remove permissions for users or roles at different levels of the hierarchy, ensuring security and controlled access within the SQL Server environment.

Examples of Permission Types:

SELECT Permission: Allows reading data from a table or view.
INSERT Permission: Permits adding data into a table.
UPDATE Permission: Grants the ability to modify existing data in a table.
DELETE Permission: Enables deleting data from a table.

Authorization Techniques:

GRANT: Assigns specific permissions to users or roles. For instance, **GRANT SELECT ON [Table] TO [User]**.
DENY: Explicitly denies a specific permission to a principal, even if it was granted earlier.
REVOKE: Removes previously granted permissions. For instance, **REVOKE SELECT ON [Table] FROM [User]**.

Permission Management:

Roles: Group permissions together to simplify management. Roles can be granted permissions, and users can be added to roles.
Stored Procedures: Control access to data by encapsulating queries within stored procedures and granting execution rights to users.
Row-Level Security (RLS): Limits rows a user can access based on conditions defined in a security policy.
Best Practices:
Least Privilege Principle: Grant only necessary permissions to users or roles.
Regular Review: Regularly review and audit permissions to ensure compliance and security.
Separation of Duties: Divide responsibilities among multiple roles to minimize the impact of potential security breaches.
Strong Authentication: Implement strong password policies and multi-factor authentication to secure logins.
By implementing these practices and understanding the nuances of permission management, organizations can ensure data security and integrity within their SQL Server environments.

10.3 Security Best Practices

Principle of Least Privilege: Ensure that users are granted only the minimum permissions required to perform their tasks. This practice reduces the risk of accidental or intentional misuse of privileges. Utilize roles and groups to manage permissions efficiently, granting access based on defined responsibilities within the organization.
Strong Authentication: Enforce strong password policies, including complexity requirements and regular password changes. Implement multifactor authentication (MFA) to add an extra layer of security. Integration with Active Directory provides centralized authentication, simplifies user management, and strengthens access control.
Regular Updates and Patches: Stay current with SQL Server updates provided by Microsoft to address security vulnerabilities. Regularly applying patches and updates is crucial to safeguard against known exploits and security flaws.
Encryption: Use encryption techniques to protect sensitive data. Implement Transparent Data Encryption (TDE) to encrypt data at rest, preventing unauthorized access to database files. Employ SSL/TLS encryption to secure data during transmission between the client and the server, mitigating the risk of data interception.
Auditing and Monitoring: Implement robust auditing mechanisms to track and log user activities, login attempts, and critical operations. Tools like SQL Server Audit facilitate the tracking of events to ensure compliance, identify suspicious activities, and aid in forensic analysis in case of security incidents.
Firewall and Network Security: Employ firewalls and network security measures to restrict access to SQL Server ports and services. Implement best practices in network security, such as using Virtual Private Networks (VPNs) or secure connections, to safeguard data transmission over networks.
Stored Procedures and Parameterization: Utilize stored procedures as a secure method for executing SQL statements, mitigating the risk of SQL injection attacks. Implement parameterized queries to prevent dynamic SQL vulnerabilities by separating data from code, reducing the likelihood of injection attacks.
Regular Backups and Recovery: Develop and execute a comprehensive backup strategy for databases and transaction logs. Regular backups safeguard against data loss due to accidental deletion, corruption, or security breaches. Ensure that recovery procedures are tested periodically to validate data integrity and restoration capabilities.
Isolation and Segmentation: Implement network segmentation and isolation measures to restrict access to SQL Server resources. Segmenting networks and implementing access controls limit exposure to unauthorized users or potential attackers, minimizing the impact of security breaches.
Limit Surface Area: Reduce the attack surface by disabling or removing unnecessary features, services, and ports in the SQL Server environment. This practice reduces the number of potential vulnerabilities and weak points that attackers could exploit to gain unauthorized access or compromise the server.
Example:

```
-- Example of creating a SQL Server login with minimal permissions
CREATE LOGIN LimitedUser WITH PASSWORD = 'StrongPassword';
GRANT CONNECT TO LimitedUser; -- Allows login to the server
CREATE USER LimitedUser FOR LOGIN LimitedUser;
GRANT SELECT ON YourTableName TO LimitedUser; -- Granting minimal read access
```

Remember, these practices should be adapted and expanded upon based on your specific security requirements and compliance standards.

10.4 Auditing and Compliance

In Microsoft SQL Server, auditing and compliance are crucial aspects of ensuring security and maintaining regulatory standards. Here's an overview along with examples:

Auditing in SQL Server:

Audit Specification: SQL Server allows the creation of audit specifications to define what actions should be audited. For instance, tracking database modifications, login attempts, schema changes, etc.

```
CREATE SERVER AUDIT SPECIFICATION LoginAttempts
FOR SERVER AUDIT AuditLogin
ADD (FAILED_LOGIN_GROUP);
```

Server Audits: Creating server-level audits to monitor and log actions at the server level, specifying destinations for audit logs (like files or the Windows Security log).

```
CREATE SERVER AUDIT AuditLogin
TO FILE (FILEPATH = 'C:\Audit\AuditLogin')
WITH (ON_FAILURE = CONTINUE);
```

Database Audits: Similarly, database-level audits can be set up to track specific activities within a database, such as data access, modifications, and schema changes.

```
CREATE DATABASE AUDIT SPECIFICATION DataChanges
FOR SERVER AUDIT AuditLogin
ADD (SELECT, INSERT, UPDATE, DELETE ON dbo.MyTable BY dbo);
```

Compliance in SQL Server:

Transparent Data Encryption (TDE): Encrypting the database files to protect data at rest.

```
ALTER DATABASE YourDatabase SET ENCRYPTION ON;
```

Row-Level Security (RLS): Implementing security policies to control access to rows in a database table based on the characteristics of the user executing a query.

```
CREATE SECURITY POLICY SalesFilter
ADD FILTER PREDICATE SalesFilteringPredicate('SalesPersonID') ON dbo.Sales
```

Dynamic Data Masking: Hiding sensitive data in the result set of a query over designated database fields.

```
ALTER TABLE dbo.CustomerInfo
ALTER COLUMN CreditCardNumber ADD MASKED WITH (FUNCTION = 'partial(4,"XXXX",0)');
```

Permission Management: Managing user permissions and roles to control access to data and objects within the SQL Server.

```
GRANT SELECT ON dbo.MyTable TO UserOrRole;
```

Examples:

Scenario: Auditing login attempts for compliance.

Solution: Create a server audit specification for failed login attempts and link it to a server audit.

Scenario: Implementing row-level security for sensitive data in the 'Finance' table.

Solution: Define a security policy with a filtering predicate to restrict access based on user roles or attributes.

Scenario: Encrypting the 'SensitiveData' database to meet compliance standards.

Solution: Enable Transparent Data Encryption for the 'SensitiveData' database.

These measures help ensure that SQL Server databases adhere to security best practices and meet various compliance regulations like GDPR, HIPAA, etc.

10.5 Exercise

Exercise 1 – MCQ

1. Which Azure service supports multifactor authentication for enhanced security?
A) Azure Active Directory (AAD)
B) Azure Key Vault
C) Azure SQL Database
D) Azure Blob Storage
2. In Azure RBAC (Role-Based Access Control), which role grants full access to all resources within a subscription?
A) Reader
B) Contributor
C) Owner
D) User Access Administrator
3. Which practice is recommended for securing sensitive data in Azure SQL Database?
A) Use weak and easily guessable passwords
B) Store encryption keys within the same database
C) Implement Transparent Data Encryption (TDE)
D) Disable all auditing and logging features
4. Which Azure service provides comprehensive audit logs and compliance reports?
A) Azure Monitor
B) Azure Sentinel
C) Azure Security Center
D) Azure Active Directory
5. Which authentication method in Azure allows users to sign in with their existing social media accounts?
A) Azure Active Directory B2C
B) Azure Active Directory Domain Services (AAD DS)
C) Azure Multi-Factor Authentication (MFA)
D) Azure AD Join
6. In Azure Storage, which permission grants the ability to read, write, delete, and list container objects but not modify access control lists (ACLs)?
A) Storage Blob Data Owner
B) Storage Blob Data Contributor
C) Storage Blob Data Reader
D) Storage Blob Delegator
7. What is the recommended method to securely manage and store secrets in Azure?
A) Store secrets in plain text files within the app's directory
B) Utilize environment variables for storing sensitive information
C) Use Azure Key Vault
D) Employ weak encryption algorithms for obfuscating secrets
8. Which Azure feature provides continuous monitoring, threat detection, and actionable insights into security issues?
A) Azure Security Center
B) Azure Sentinel
C) Azure Policy
D) Azure Identity Protection
9. Which Azure service enables users to authenticate with Azure AD credentials to access resources like virtual machines (VMs)?
A) Azure Active Directory Domain Services (AAD DS)
B) Azure AD Join
C) Azure Active Directory B2C
D) Azure Multi-Factor Authentication (MFA)
10. What is the principle behind the "least privilege" concept in Azure's security model?
A) Granting excessive permissions to all users
B) Assigning users permissions based on their role requirements
C) Providing blanket access to all resources
D) Assigning administrative privileges to all users

Exercise 2 – True/ False

1. Azure Active Directory (AAD) supports only multi-factor authentication for enhanced security.

2. Azure Role-Based Access Control (RBAC) allows fine-grained access management by assigning permissions to users at the subscription level only.
3. Enabling Azure Security Center ensures protection against threats and vulnerabilities, providing recommendations but not taking any automated actions to mitigate issues.
4. Azure provides native tools for comprehensive audit logging and monitoring, but external solutions are required for compliance reporting.
5. Azure Active Directory (AAD) supports authentication methods like OAuth, SAML, and OpenID Connect for diverse application needs.
6. Azure Resource Manager (ARM) allows role-based access control at the resource group level for streamlined permission assignment.
7. Encrypting sensitive data at rest is recommended in Azure, with options like Azure Disk Encryption and Azure Storage Service Encryption available.
8. Azure Security Center provides continuous monitoring, threat detection, and automated response to security threats without manual intervention.
9. Azure supports multiple authentication methods, including certificates, managed identities, and federated identities, offering flexibility to applications.
10. Azure Active Directory allows administrators to define custom roles with specific permissions tailored to the organization's requirements.

Exercise 3 – Fill in the blanks

1. ____________ is a process that verifies the identity of a user or application attempting to access Azure resources.
2. In Azure, role-based ____________ enables granting granular access to resources based on predefined roles.
3. Implementing ____________ is crucial to prevent unauthorized access and secure Azure services and data.
4. Azure Security Centre provides continuous ____________ to identify and remediate potential vulnerabilities in resources.
5. Multi-factor ____________ adds an extra layer of security by requiring users to provide multiple forms of verification.
6. ____________ in Azure allows setting fine-grained access controls, specifying who can access specific resources.
7. Azure Key Vault helps safeguard cryptographic ____________ such as keys, secrets, and certificates used by cloud applications.
8. Azure Active Directory (AAD) supports various ____________ modes, including password hash synchronization and pass-through authentication.
9. Regular ____________ in Azure involves reviewing access logs, assessing security configurations, and identifying compliance gaps.
10. Azure Policy allows defining and enforcing ____________ across Azure subscriptions to ensure compliance and governance.

Exercise 4 – One word answer

1. What is the default authentication method in Azure Active Directory?
2. What is the role-based access control mechanism in Azure called?
3. Which encryption method is recommended for data at rest in Azure Storage?
4. What Azure service provides compliance reports and auditing capabilities?
5. What protocol is often used for user authentication in Azure services?
6. What is the fundamental unit of access control in Azure's RBAC?
7. What type of scanning helps identify potential security vulnerabilities in Azure resources?
8. What Azure feature helps organizations comply with regulatory standards like GDPR?
9. What authentication mechanism allows users to log in using their social media accounts?
10. What Azure feature allows fine-grained control over access to specific resources?

Exercise 5 – Small answer

1. What Azure service facilitates the use of Azure Active Directory (AAD) for managing user identities and access?
2. Define Role-Based Access Control (RBAC) in Azure and its primary purpose.
3. Name one recommended security best practice for securing Azure Virtual Machines (VMs).
4. What Azure service provides comprehensive auditing and compliance features for tracking user activity and meeting regulatory requirements?

5. Name a method used for securing access to Azure Storage accounts, providing a secure connection over the internet.
6. What are the different types of roles available in Azure RBAC?
7. How does Azure Active Directory (AAD) integration enhance security in Azure services?
8. Explain the primary purpose of Azure Key Vault in maintaining security.
9. What role does Azure Security Center play in Azure's security ecosystem?
10. Name one compliance standard supported by Azure for data privacy and protection.

Exercise 6 – Long answer

1. Explain various authentication modes available in Azure, including Azure Active Directory, Azure Multi-Factor Authentication, and service principal authentication. Compare and contrast these modes, highlighting their use cases and security implications.
2. Describe the role of RBAC in Azure's authorization framework. Explain the concept of role assignments and their significance in managing access to Azure resources. Provide examples of scenarios where fine-grained access control via RBAC is crucial.
3. Elaborate on encryption methods and data protection mechanisms available in Azure. Discuss how Azure Key Vault and Azure Disk Encryption contribute to securing sensitive data. Provide examples of scenarios where encryption is paramount.
4. Explain the concept of IAM in Azure and its role in controlling access to resources. Discuss how Azure Active Directory (AAD) manages identities and how it integrates with Azure services for authentication and authorization.
5. Explain the importance of compliance and adherence to regulatory standards in Azure. Discuss how Azure services facilitate compliance with regulations such as GDPR, HIPAA, and ISO standards. Detail the auditing mechanisms available for compliance monitoring.

Answer

Exercise 1:
Answer: 1: A, 2: C, 3: C, 4: C, 5: A, 6: B, 7: C, 8: B, 9: B, 10: B
Exercise 2:
Answer: 1: False, 2: False, 3: True, 4: False, 5: True, 6: True 7: True, 8: False, 9: True, 10: True
Exercise 3:
Answer: 1: Authentication,2: authorization, 3: security, 4: monitoring, 5: authentication, 6: Role-based access control (RBAC), 7: keys, secrets, 8: authentication, 9: auditing, 10: governance policies
Exercise 4:
Answer: 1: Azure AD,2: RBAC, 3: AES, 4: Azure Sentinel, 5: OAuth, 6: Role, 7: Vulnerability, 8: Compliance, 9: Social, 10: Policies.

ONLINE RESOURCES

Practice Paper
Link: https://forms.office.com/r/iGiv3tFLpS?origin=lprLink.
QR Code:

Chapter 11: Business Intelligence with SQL Server

11.1 SQL Server Integration Services (SSIS)

Business Intelligence Development Studio is the environment that can be used to develop packages for data Extraction, Transfer and Load (ETL) in integration services. It can be used to create simple and complex packages.
Basically, integration services is a solution of one or more packages. It is a much richer feature of Business Intelligence Development Studio.
SQL Server Integration Services (SSIS) is a powerful data integration and workflow tool offered by Microsoft as part of the SQL Server suite. It facilitates the extraction, transformation, and loading (ETL) of data from various sources into a target destination, often for business intelligence (BI) purposes.

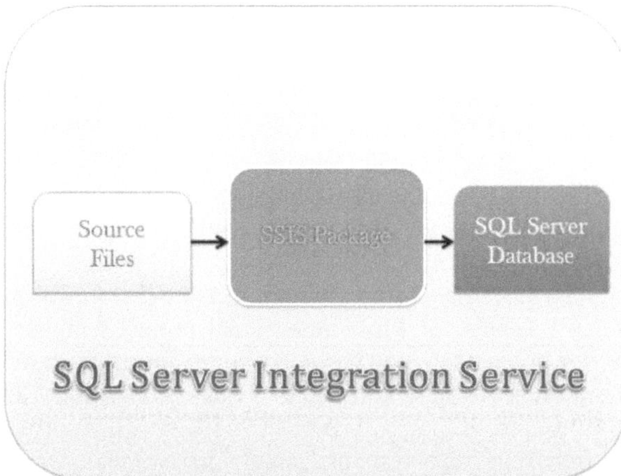

Key Features and Components:
ETL Capabilities: SSIS enables the extraction of data from various sources (databases, flat files, APIs), transforming it based on business rules, and loading it into a data warehouse or other destinations.
Control Flow: SSIS packages contain control flow elements to define workflow logic, such as conditional execution, loops, and parallelism.
Data Flow: The Data Flow Task within SSIS packages manages the flow of data between sources and destinations. It supports transformations like merging, sorting, aggregating, and data type conversion.
Connectivity: It provides native connectors for various data sources (SQL Server, Oracle, Excel, etc.) and supports OLE DB, ODBC, ADO.NET, and other data access providers.
Scripting: SSIS allows integration of custom scripts using languages like C# or VB.NET for advanced transformations or custom components.
Deployment and Execution: SSIS packages can be deployed to SQL Server, executed through SQL Server Agent, or scheduled using SQL Server Integration Services Catalogs.
Business Intelligence with SSIS:
Data Warehousing: SSIS is widely used for populating data warehouses from different sources, enabling efficient analysis and reporting.
ETL Pipelines: It forms the backbone of ETL pipelines, facilitating the movement of data between operational systems and BI repositories.
Data Cleansing and Transformation: SSIS provides tools for data cleansing, ensuring consistency, quality, and standardization across datasets.
Real-time Analytics: By continuously moving and transforming data, SSIS supports real-time analytics and reporting for timely business insights.
Automated Processes: It enables automation of repetitive data tasks, reducing manual intervention and ensuring data accuracy.
Example:
Scenario: Extracting data from different databases, transforming it, and loading it into a data warehouse for analysis.
Solution: Create an SSIS package with data flow tasks to extract data from various sources using corresponding connectors, apply transformations (cleaning, aggregating), and load it into a centralized data warehouse.

SQL Server Agent Job: Schedule the SSIS package as an SQL Server Agent job to run at specific intervals or events, ensuring regular updates of the data warehouse.
SSIS plays a pivotal role in building robust data integration solutions for business intelligence, enabling organizations to make informed decisions by providing reliable and timely access to data.

11.2 SQL Server Analysis Services (SSAS)

Analysis Services is an analytical data engine (VertiPaq) used in decision support and business analytics. It provides enterprise-grade semantic data models for business reports and client applications such as Power BI, Excel, Reporting Services reports, and other data visualization tools.
Installed as an on-premises or virtual machine server instance, SQL Server Analysis Services supports tabular models at all compatibility levels (depending on version), multidimensional models, data mining, and Power Pivot for SharePoint.
SQL Server Analysis Services (SSAS) is a part of Microsoft's SQL Server suite, designed for business intelligence (BI) and analytics. It enables the creation of Online Analytical Processing (OLAP) solutions and data mining functionalities.

SQL Server Analysis Services workflow

A common workflow includes installing a SQL Server Analysis Services instance, creating a tabular or multidimensional data model, deploying the model as a database to a server instance, processing the database to load it with data, and then assigning permissions to allow data access. When ready to go, the data model is accessed by any client application supporting Analysis Services as a data source.
To create a model, use Visual Studio with Analysis Services projects extension, also known as SQL Server Data Tools or simply SSDT, choosing either a Tabular or Multidimensional project template. The project template contains folders for all of the objects needed in a model. You can use wizards to create all of the basic elements, such as data sources, data source views, dimensions, cubes, and roles. Visual Studio and DevOps supports efficient CI/CD pipelines.
Models are populated with data from other data systems, usually data warehouses hosted on a SQL Server or Oracle relational database engine (Tabular models support more data source types). Models specify query objects, calculations, and KPIs that encapsulate business logic.
To use a model, deploy it to a server instance and make it available to authorized users who connect through Excel or other applications.

Key Components:

Multidimensional Models (OLAP): SSAS supports multidimensional data models, providing data cubes and dimensions for efficient querying and analysis.
Tabular Models: It also offers tabular models, representing data in tables similar to relational databases, optimized for in-memory analytics.

Capabilities and Features:

Data Cubes: SSAS allows the creation of data cubes for aggregating and summarizing data for faster querying and analysis.
Dimensional Modeling: It facilitates building dimensions and measures for slicing and dicing data efficiently.
MDX and DAX: Supports Multidimensional Expressions (MDX) for multidimensional models and Data Analysis Expressions (DAX) for tabular models.
Data Mining: Includes functionalities for predictive analysis and data mining to discover patterns and insights in data.
Hierarchies and KPIs: Enables the creation of hierarchies and Key Performance Indicators (KPIs) for better data visualization and monitoring.

Benefits:

Performance: By pre-aggregating data in cubes or in-memory models, SSAS enhances query performance.
Advanced Analytics: Allows users to perform complex analytical operations and data mining to gain deeper insights.
Scalability: Can handle large volumes of data, offering scalability options for growing businesses.
Visualization Tools Integration: Integrates with visualization tools like Power BI, Excel, etc., for data representation.

Example Scenario:

Scenario: A retail company wants to analyse sales data to improve inventory management and customer experience.
Solution: Use SSAS to create a multidimensional model with sales data cubes. Define dimensions like time, products, and regions, along with measures like sales revenue and quantity sold. Implement KPIs to monitor sales performance. Leverage data mining capabilities to identify customer buying patterns for better inventory forecasting.
SSAS plays a pivotal role in extracting valuable insights from large datasets, enabling businesses to make informed decisions and gain a competitive edge in their respective industries.

11.3 SQL Server Reporting Services (SSRS)

SQL Server Reporting Services (SSRS) is a comprehensive reporting platform within the SQL Server suite that facilitates the creation, management, and delivery of reports.

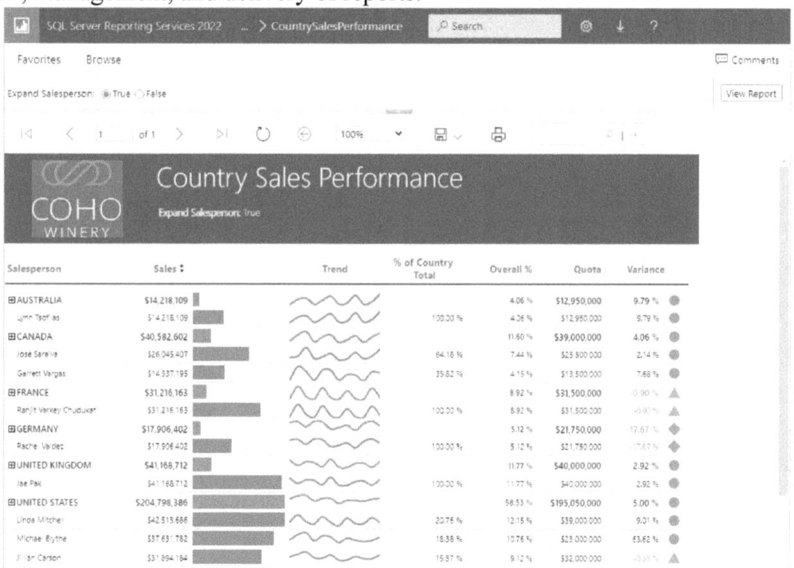

Key Components:

Report Server: The central server that hosts and manages reports, providing a web-based interface for report management.

Report Builder: An intuitive, stand-alone tool for building and customizing reports without the need for extensive programming knowledge.

Report Designer (Visual Studio Data Tools): A more advanced environment within Visual Studio for developing sophisticated reports and managing complex data sources.

Capabilities:

Report Creation: SSRS allows the creation of various types of reports (tabular, matrix, charts, etc.) using data from SQL Server databases, OLAP cubes, or other sources.

Parameterized Reports: Users can create reports that accept parameters, enabling dynamic report generation based on user input.

Data Visualization: Provides a range of visualization options to present data effectively, including graphs, charts, and maps.

Scheduling and Subscriptions: Automate report generation and distribution by scheduling reports or setting up subscriptions for specific users or groups.

Security and Access Control: SSRS offers robust security features to control access to reports and data sources, ensuring data confidentiality and integrity.

Interactive Reporting: Allows end-users to interact with reports by drilling down, sorting, and filtering data for deeper insights.

Create, deploy, and manage reports

The SSRS solution flexibly delivers the right information to the right users. Users can consume the reports in a web browser on their computer or mobile device, or via email.

SQL Server Reporting Services offers an updated suite of products:

Paginated reports brought up to date, so you can create modern-looking reports, with updated tools and new features for creating them.

A modern web portal you can view in any modern browser. In the new portal, you can organize and display paginated Reporting Services reports and KPIs. You can also store Excel workbooks on the portal.

Paginated reports

Reporting Services is associated with paginated reports, ideal for fixed-layout documents optimized for printing, such as PDF and Word files.
That core BI workload still exists today, so we've modernized it.
We updated all the default styles and color palettes, so by default you create reports with a new minimalist modern style.
We updated the Parameter pane, so you can arrange parameters however you want.
You can export to new formats such as PowerPoint. Reporting Services visualizations in PowerPoint are live and editable, not just screenshots.
You can create a hybrid Power BI/Reporting Services experience: Rather than recreating your on-premises Reporting Services reports in Power BI, you can pin visuals from those reports to your Power BI dashboards. Then you can monitor everything in one place on your Power BI dashboard.

Web portal

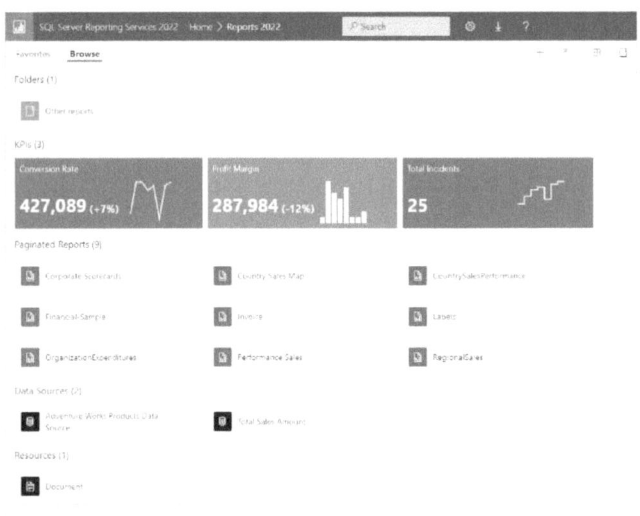

For end users of Reporting Services, the front door is a modern web portal you can view in most browsers. You can access all your Reporting Services reports and KPIs in the new portal. KPIs can surface key business metrics at a glance in the browser, without having to open a report.
The new web portal is a complete rewrite of Report Manager. Now it's a single-page, standards-based HTML5 app, which modern browsers are optimized for: Microsoft Edge, Internet Explorer 10 and 11, Chrome, Firefox, Safari, and all the major browsers.

Example Usage:
Consider a scenario in a retail company:

Problem: The retail company needs a detailed monthly sales report categorized by region, product type, and sales channel.

Solution with SSRS:

Data Gathering: Connect SSRS to the SQL Server database containing sales data.

Report Creation: Develop a report template using Report Builder or Report Designer, including parameters for time range, region, and product type.

Visualization: Include charts and graphs to present sales performance visually.

Parameterization: Enable users to select specific time frames, regions, or product types for tailored reports.

Scheduling: Schedule the report to run automatically at the end of each month and distribute it to relevant stakeholders via email or a shared folder.

SSRS facilitates the creation of detailed, interactive reports that offer insights into various business aspects, enabling informed decision-making.

11.4 Exercise

Exercise 1 – MCQ

1. Which SQL Server component is primarily used for data integration, including extracting, transforming, and loading (ETL) operations?
a) SSRS
b) SSAS
c) SSIS
d) SSMS

2. Which SQL Server service is focused on creating and managing multidimensional data models and online analytical processing (OLAP) cubes?
a) SSRS
b) SSIS
c) SSAS
d) SSMS

3. Which SQL Server feature provides tools for creating interactive, tabular, graphical reports, and dashboards?
a) SSAS
b) SSRS
c) SSIS
d) SQL Profiler

4. What does SSIS stand for in the context of SQL Server?
a) SQL Server Information Services
b) SQL Server Integration Services
c) SQL Server Integration System
d) SQL Server Interactive Services

5. Which of the following is NOT a feature of SQL Server Analysis Services (SSAS)?
a) Data mining
b) Tabular model
c) Reporting
d) Multidimensional model

6. SSRS in SQL Server stands for:
a) SQL Server Report Services
b) SQL Server Reporting Services
c) SQL Server Reliable Services
d) SQL Server Remote Services

7. Which SQL Server service specializes in creating data visualizations and predictive models for discovering patterns in data?
a) SSRS
b) SSAS
c) SSIS
d) SQL Profiler

8. In SQL Server, what is the primary function of SSIS?
a) Data analysis
b) Data integration and ETL

c) Report generation
d) Data mining
9. Which SQL Server component is used to create, deploy, and manage reports in various formats?
a) SSAS
b) SSRS
c) SSIS
d) SQL Agent
10. Which SQL Server service is used for creating data cubes and performing multidimensional analysis?
a) SSRS
b) SSAS
c) SSIS
d) SQL Server Browser

Exercise 2 – True/ False

1. SQL Server Integration Services (SSIS) supports the extraction, transformation, and loading (ETL) of data from various sources into SQL Server databases.
2. SQL Server Analysis Services (SSAS) is primarily used for creating and managing reports, dashboards, and scorecards.
3. SSRS allows users to design and generate reports using data from SQL Server databases but does not support data visualization.
4. SSIS is commonly used for real-time analytics and provides functionalities for predictive analysis.
5. SQL Server Analysis Services offers both Multidimensional Expressions (MDX) and Data Mining Expressions (DMX) for querying and analyzing data.
6. SSRS supports various report formats, including tabular reports, matrix reports, and free-form reports.
7. SQL Server Integration Services provides tools and services for data cleansing, making it suitable for maintaining data quality.
8. SSAS supports the creation of OLAP cubes, allowing users to perform multidimensional analysis of data.
9. SSIS is exclusively used for data warehousing and doesn't support integration with other systems or applications.
10. SQL Server Reporting Services provides features for scheduling and delivering reports via email or to a file share.

Exercise 3 – Fill in the blanks

1. SQL Server Integration Services (SSIS) is primarily used for ____________ purposes, enabling the extraction, transformation, and loading (ETL) of data from various sources into the SQL Server database for analysis and reporting.
2. SQL Server Analysis Services (SSAS) provides ____________ modeling capabilities, allowing users to create multidimensional models for analyzing complex data and generating business insights.
3. In SQL Server Reporting Services (SSRS), the ____________ is a centralized repository to manage and store report definitions, data sources, datasets, and other report-related resources.
4. SSIS offers a wide range of ____________ that facilitate the transformation of data during ETL processes, such as data conversion, conditional split, and merge join.
5. The ____________ in SSAS defines the structure of multidimensional cubes, including dimensions, measures, hierarchies, and aggregations.
6. SSRS provides various ____________ that aid in the creation of visually appealing and interactive reports, allowing users to add charts, tables, and parameters to reports.
7. One of the core components of SSIS is the ____________, which orchestrates the workflow and execution of tasks within a package.
8. In SSAS, the ____________ serves as a pre-aggregated summary of data to enhance query performance when analyzing large datasets.
9. SSRS allows users to schedule report execution and delivery through ____________, ensuring that reports are generated and sent to specific recipients at predefined times.
10. SSIS offers robust ____________ that enable connections to diverse data sources, including SQL Server, Excel, flat files, and cloud-based platforms.

Exercise 4 – One word answer

1. What does the "I" stand for in SSIS?

2. What does the "A" stand for in SSAS?
3. What does the "R" stand for in SSRS?
4. What does the "E" stand for in ETL processes within SSIS?
5. What is the term used to describe a multidimensional data structure in SSAS?
6. What does the acronym OLAP represent in SSAS?
7. What does SSRS use to retrieve data for reports?
8. In SSIS, what is the name of the component that defines the movement and transformation of data?
9. What does the acronym KPI stand for in SSAS?
10. Which tool in SSRS allows users to create reports without writing code?

Exercise 5 – Small answer

1. What is the primary function of SQL Server Integration Services (SSIS) in a BI environment?
2. Define SQL Server Analysis Services (SSAS) and its core purpose within a business intelligence framework.
3. Explain the primary role of SQL Server Reporting Services (SSRS) in delivering insights to stakeholders.
4. How does SSIS facilitate data integration across various sources within an organization?
5. Define the concept of cubes in SQL Server Analysis Services (SSAS) and their significance in data analysis.
6. What are the common methods for deploying reports using SQL Server Reporting Services (SSRS)?
7. Briefly describe the Extract, Transform, Load (ETL) process in SSIS and its importance in data warehousing.
8. What role does Online Analytical Processing (OLAP) play in SQL Server Analysis Services (SSAS) for data analysis?
9. How do report parameters enhance the functionality of reports created using SQL Server Reporting Services (SSRS)?
10. Highlight a key difference between SSAS Multidimensional and Tabular models in SQL Server Analysis Services (SSAS).

Exercise 6 – Long answer

1. Explain the role of SSIS in SQL Server's Business Intelligence. Discuss the key features and functionalities of SSIS, citing examples of scenarios where SSIS is instrumental in ETL processes.
2. Outline the steps involved in developing an SSIS package. Elaborate on the various tools, tasks, and data flow components available in SSIS, and describe their functionalities within the context of package development.
3. Define the ETL process in the context of SSIS. Describe the stages of Extraction, Transformation, and Loading (ETL) and how SSIS facilitates these processes. Provide examples of transformations used in SSIS.
4. Explain the different data flow tasks and components available in SSIS. Discuss their specific purposes and how they contribute to building an efficient data flow pipeline within SSIS packages.
5. Detail the role and importance of SSAS in Business Intelligence. Describe the multidimensional and tabular models within SSAS, highlighting their differences and suitable use cases.
6. Explain the concept of a multidimensional model in SSAS. Describe cubes, dimensions, measures, and hierarchies, illustrating how these elements are created and used for analysis.
7. Discuss the tabular model in SSAS and its advantages. Outline the process of creating a tabular model, including data modeling, relationships, and the implementation of DAX expressions.
8. Define SSRS and its significance in Business Intelligence. Describe the components of SSRS reports and the report development lifecycle within SSRS.
9. Explain the steps involved in developing reports using SSRS. Discuss various report design elements, visualization options, and parameters available in SSRS for creating interactive reports.
10. Illustrate a scenario where integration between SSIS, SSAS, and SSRS is beneficial in a Business Intelligence solution. Describe the data flow from extraction through transformation, to analysis, and finally, report generation using these services.

Answer

Exercise 1:

Answer: 1: c, 2: c, 3: b, 4: b, 5: c, 6: b, 7: b, 8: b, 9: b, 10: b

Exercise 2:

Answer: 1: True, 2: False, 3: False, 4: False, 5: True, 6: True 7: True, 8: True, 9: False, 10: True

Exercise 3:

Answer: 1: data integration,2: data mining, 3: Report Server, 4: data transformation tasks, 5: cube schema, 6: report elements, 7: control flow, 8: aggregate table, 9: subscriptions, 10: connection managers

Exercise 4:
Answer: 1: Integration,2: Analysis, 3: Reporting, 4: Extraction, 5: Cube, 6: Online Analytical Processing, 7: Data Source, 8: Data Flow, 9: Key Performance Indicator, 10: Report Builder.

ONLINE RESOURCES

Practice Paper
Link: https://forms.office.com/r/jvrBb8FysX?origin=lprLink.
QR Code:

Chapter 12: Working with Azure SQL Database

12.1 Overview of Azure SQL Database

Azure SQL Database is a cloud-based relational database service offered by Microsoft as part of the Azure suite. It's based on the SQL Server Database Engine but operates as a Platform as a Service (PaaS) in the cloud.

Azure SQL Database is always running on the latest stable version of the SQL Server database engine and patched OS with 99.99% availability. PaaS capabilities built into Azure SQL Database enable you to focus on the domain-specific database administration and optimization activities that are critical for your business. With Azure SQL Database, you can create a highly available and high-performance data storage layer for the applications and solutions in Azure. SQL Database can be the right choice for a variety of modern cloud applications because it enables you to process both relational data and nonrelational structures, such as graphs, JSON, spatial, and XML.

Key Features:

Fully Managed: Azure SQL Database is a fully managed service, handling maintenance, updates, backups, and security, reducing administrative overhead.

Scalability: Offers various service tiers, allowing users to scale resources (compute and storage) based on demand without downtime.

High Availability: Provides built-in high availability with automatic backups, automated patching, and geo-replication for disaster recovery.

Security: Implements advanced security measures such as encryption at rest and in transit, threat detection, and access control to protect data.

Compatibility: Supports compatibility with on-premises SQL Server, allowing smooth migration and integration with existing applications.

Intelligence: Integrates AI-driven features for performance tuning, query optimization, and intelligent insights into database operations.

Developer Tools: Offers tools like Azure Data Studio, Azure CLI, and PowerShell for efficient management and development.

Purchasing models

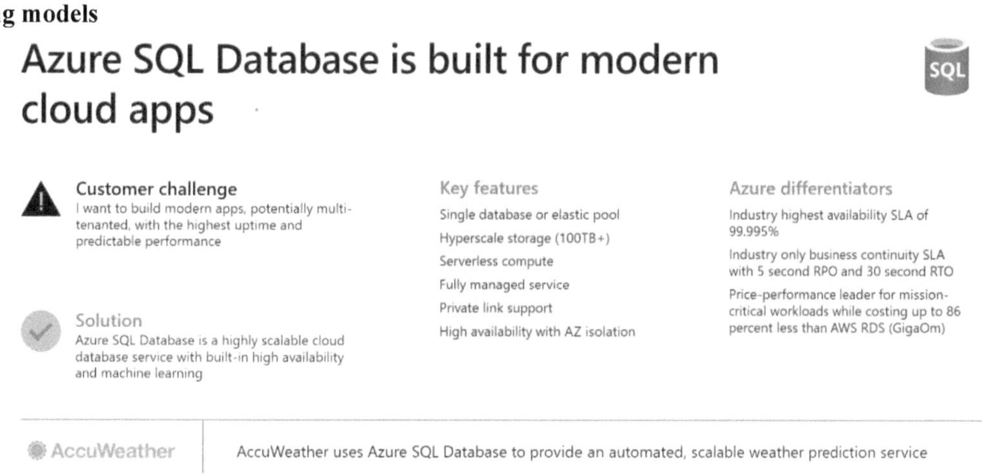

SQL Database offers the following purchasing models:

The vCore-based purchasing model lets you choose the number of vCores, the amount of memory, and the amount and speed of storage. The vCore-based purchasing model also allows you to use Azure Hybrid Benefit for SQL Server to gain cost savings by leveraging your existing SQL Server licenses.

The DTU-based purchasing model offers a blend of compute, memory, and I/O resources in three service tiers, to support light to heavy database workloads. Compute sizes within each tier provide a different mix of these resources, to which you can add additional storage resources.

Service tiers

The vCore-based purchasing model offers three service tiers:

The General-Purpose service tier is designed for common workloads. It offers budget-oriented balanced compute and storage options.

The Business-Critical service tier is designed for OLTP applications with high transaction rates and low latency I/O requirements. It offers the highest resilience to failures by using several isolated replicas.

The Hyperscale service tier is designed for most business workloads. Hyperscale provides great flexibility and high performance with independently scalable compute and storage resources. It offers higher resilience to failures by allowing configuration of more than one isolated database replica.

The DTU-based purchasing model offers two service tiers:

The Standard service tier is designed for common workloads. It offers budget-oriented balanced compute and storage options.

The Premium service tier is designed for OLTP applications with high transaction rates and low latency I/O requirements. It offers the highest resilience to failures by using several isolated replicas.

Advantages:

Cost-Efficiency: Pay-as-you-go model, allowing users to scale resources as needed, reducing costs associated with over-provisioning.

Scalability and Performance: Easily scale resources up or down to handle varying workloads, ensuring optimal performance.

Reliability and Availability: Built-in redundancies and disaster recovery options ensure high availability and reliability.

Security and Compliance: Adheres to various compliance standards and offers robust security features for data protection.

Use Cases:

Modern Web and Mobile Apps: Ideal for applications requiring a scalable, low-latency backend database.

Line-of-Business Applications: Supports mission-critical applications that require high availability and reliability.

Development and Testing: Provides an efficient environment for development, testing, and prototyping.

Analytics and Reporting: Enables the storage and analysis of large volumes of data for business insights.

Azure SQL Database provides a robust and scalable cloud-based database solution, catering to diverse application requirements while ensuring high availability, security, and performance.

12.2 Deploying Databases to Azure

Deploying databases to Azure involves the process of migrating or creating databases on Microsoft's Azure cloud platform. This transition offers several advantages, such as scalability, reliability, and accessibility.

Before deploying your project to Azure App Service, it's crucial to transfer your project's database to Azure SQL Database. Azure SQL Database stands as a powerful database-as-a-service offering, delivering intelligent, scalable, and cloud-based database services with comprehensive compatibility with the SQL Server engine. To ensure your Sitefinity website database operates seamlessly within Azure SQL Database, follow these steps:

Setting Up Your SQL Server

Before deploying your Sitefinity website's database to the cloud, you'll need a dedicated SQL server to host it. Follow these steps to create a new SQL server if you don't already have one:

Access the Azure Portal.

Use the search bar at the top to find 'SQL Server.'

Select 'SQL Servers' from the search results.

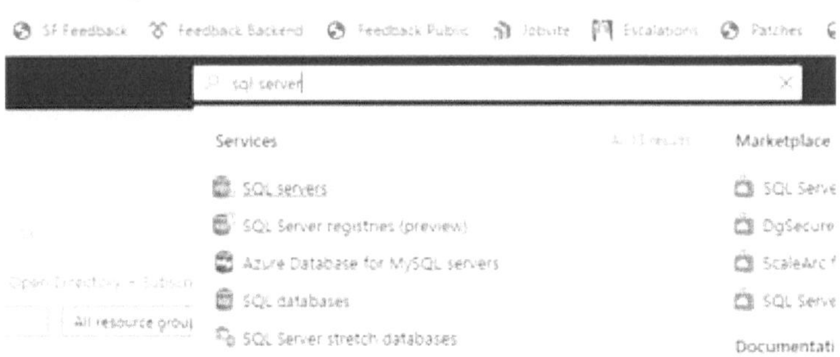

Click on the 'Add' button.

Fill in the required information:

- Server name: Provide a name for your new SQL Server.
- Server admin login: Your server admin username.
- Password: Set a secure password.
- Subscription: Choose an existing Microsoft Azure subscription.
- Resource group: Select an existing group or create a new one.

Location: Choose a location for optimal performance based on website traffic.

Note: Keep a record of these details; you'll need them later to connect to your server.

Click 'Create.'

Once created, your SQL server will appear in the list for your Azure subscription. If it doesn't immediately show up, use the 'Refresh' button to check for updates.

Deploying Your Database to Azure SQL

Once your SQL Server has been created, you can now proceed with deploying your website database to Azure SQL Database. The process is facilitated in your local installation of SQL Server Management Studio (SSMS). You must connect to your SQL server in Microsoft Azure and deploy your local database there. Follow these steps:

Launch SQL Server Management Studio (SSMS) on the machine where your website's database is restored.

Locate your database in SSMS, right-click on it, and choose 'Tasks' » 'Deploy Database to Microsoft Azure SQL Database.'

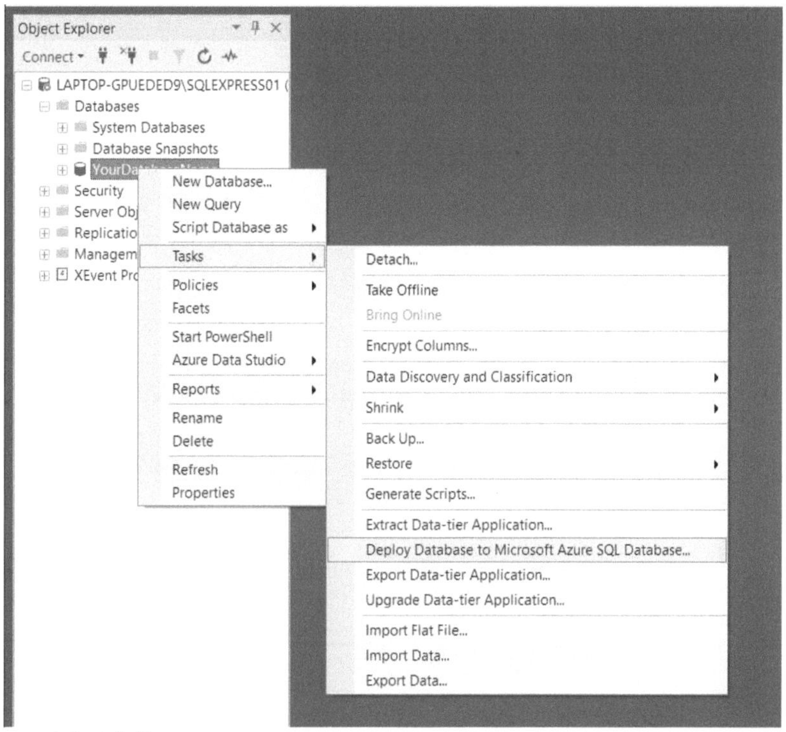

Click 'Next' on the prompt that follows.

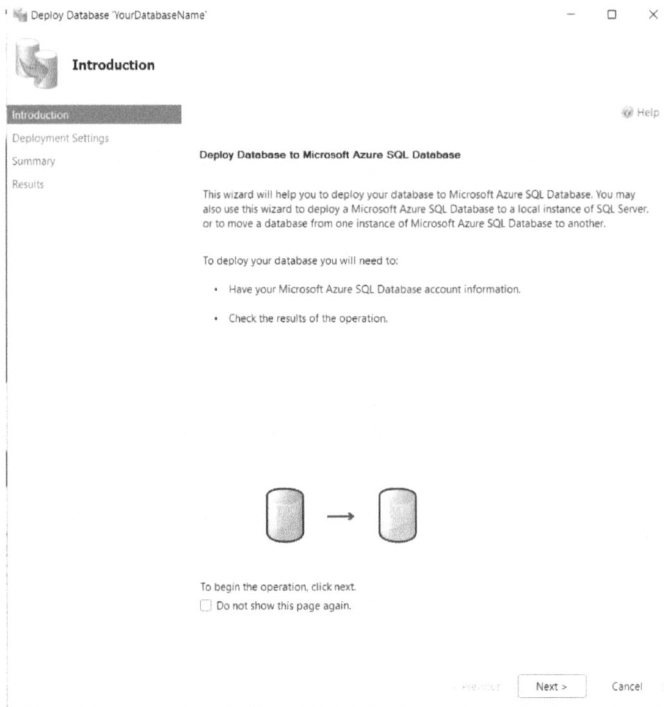

Fill in your Azure SQL server connection details. Use the information you supplied while creating the SQL server in Azure. If you had an existing SQL server in your Azure subscription, input its details instead.

Click 'Connect' when finished.

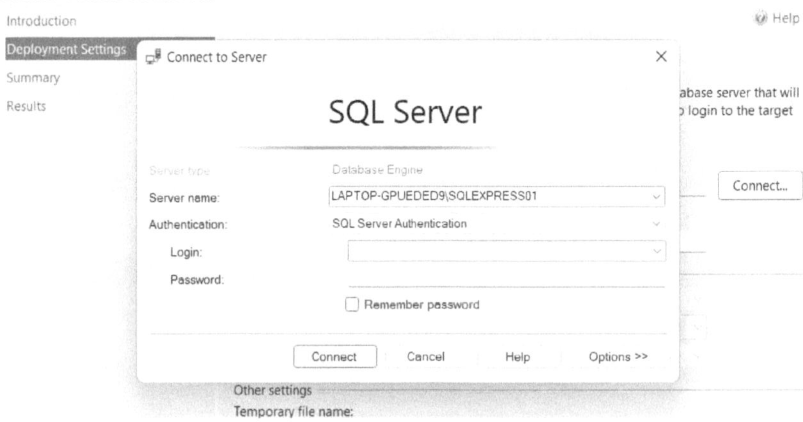

If you haven't added a firewall rule in your Azure account allowing communication from your local dev machine's IP, the wizard in SSMS lets you configure this without leaving the interface. Sign in with your Azure account, and add a firewall rule for your IP address.

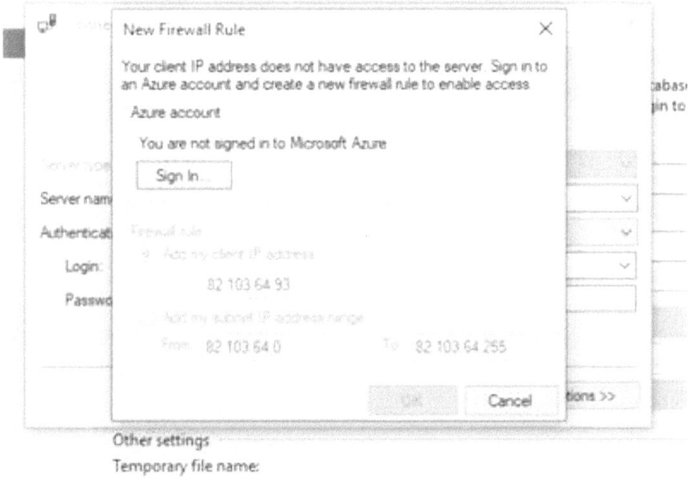

The subsequent screen enables you to configure your Azure SQL Database parameters, including the database's size and performance settings. Recommended settings for Sitefinity are as follows:

Edition: Standard

Maximum database size: 50 GB

Service objective: S2 NOTE: These settings are the recommended minimum for a Sitefinity database. For detailed configurations and pricing, refer to Azure SQL Database pricing.

Click 'Next.'

Review the configured options on the summary screen and click 'Finish' to begin the deployment process.

Once deployment finishes, click 'Close' on the completion screen.

Key Concepts:

Azure SQL Database: A fully managed relational database service offered by Microsoft Azure, providing SQL databases as a service.

Azure SQL Managed Instance: A fully managed SQL Server database engine that provides a broad range of features for migrating databases to Azure without rearchitecting applications.

Azure Database for MySQL/PostgreSQL: Managed database services for open-source databases, offering flexibility and scalability.

Process Overview:

Assessment: Evaluate the existing on-premises or cloud-based databases to determine the best migration strategy, considering database size, complexity, and performance requirements.

Migration Planning: Choose the appropriate Azure database service (SQL Database, Managed Instance, MySQL, PostgreSQL) based on compatibility, performance, and cost considerations.

Data Migration: Use Azure Data Migration Services or other tools to migrate data to Azure databases while minimizing downtime and ensuring data integrity.

Application Reconfiguration: Modify application settings or connection strings to point to the new Azure database instances.

Testing and Validation: Perform extensive testing to ensure that applications are functioning correctly with the migrated databases.

Optimization and Scaling: Leverage Azure's scalability features to optimize database performance and scale resources based on demand.

Benefits:

Scalability: Azure provides scalable resources that can accommodate varying workload demands.

Security: Azure offers robust security measures to protect databases, including encryption, firewall rules, and advanced threat detection.

Reliability: High availability and disaster recovery options ensure databases are accessible and protected against data loss.

Cost-Effectiveness: Pay-as-you-go pricing models and resource scaling options help optimize costs.

Example Scenario:

Consider a company with an on-premises SQL Server database for customer information.

Deployment Steps:

Assess database compatibility with Azure SQL Database.

Use Azure Database Migration Service to migrate the on-premises SQL Server database to Azure SQL Database.
Configure firewall rules and security settings for the Azure SQL Database.
Update application connection strings to point to the Azure SQL Database.
Validate data integrity and application functionality post-migration.
This deployment to Azure enables the company to leverage cloud-based advantages like scalability, security, and manageability for their customer database.
Successful deployment to Azure involves careful planning, execution, and validation to ensure a smooth transition of databases to the cloud environment.

12.3 Managing Azure SQL Database

Azure SQL Database is a cloud-based relational database service provided by Microsoft in Azure. Managing your Azure SQL Database involves various tasks such as configuring settings, optimizing performance, monitoring, and security management. Below are key aspects of managing Azure SQL Database:

Configuration and Scaling:

- **Pricing Tiers:** Azure SQL Database offers various performance tiers. Evaluate and choose the appropriate tier based on your workload needs.
- **Scaling:** Consider scaling options like vertical scaling (increasing the database size or performance) or horizontal scaling (using sharding or partitioning).

Monitoring and Performance Optimization:

- **Query Performance:** Monitor query performance using tools like Azure Monitor or Query Store. Optimize slow queries by creating appropriate indexes and optimizing SQL queries.
- **Performance Recommendations:** Utilize Azure Advisor for performance recommendations and insights to optimize database performance.

Backup and Recovery:

- **Automated Backups:** Enable automated backups to ensure regular database backups.
- **Point-in-time Restore:** Configure point-in-time restore to recover the database to a specific point in time.

Security and Access Control:

- **Firewall Configuration:** Configure Azure Firewall rules to control access to your database.
- **Role-Based Access Control (RBAC):** Use RBAC to manage access rights for different users or roles.
- **Data Encryption:** Implement encryption for data at rest and data in transit.

High Availability and Disaster Recovery:

- **Geo-Replication:** Set up geo-replication for disaster recovery purposes, ensuring data redundancy in different geographic regions.
- **Failover Groups:** Configure failover groups for high availability in case of a regional outage.

Troubleshooting and Diagnostics:

- **Azure Monitor:** Monitor database performance metrics, set alerts, and diagnose issues using Azure Monitor.
- **Query Store:** Analyze query performance trends and history using Query Store.

Cost Management:

- **Cost Analysis:** Regularly review cost analytics and optimize resource utilization to manage costs effectively.

Automation and Scripting:

- **Azure Automation:** Leverage Azure Automation to automate routine management tasks using PowerShell or Azure CLI scripts.

Lifecycle Management:

- **Database Lifecycle Management (DLM):** Implement strategies for version control, continuous integration, and deployment to ensure efficient database lifecycle management.

By proactively managing these aspects of Azure SQL Database, you can ensure optimal performance, security, and reliability for your applications and data.

Create a server

To create a server using the Azure portal, create a new server resource from Azure Marketplace. Alternatively, you can create the server when you deploy an Azure SQL Database.

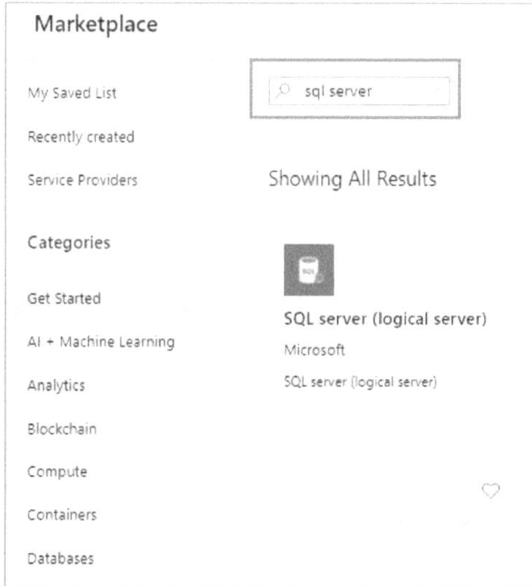

Create a blank or sample database

To create a single Azure SQL Database using the Azure portal, choose the Azure SQL Database resource in Azure Marketplace. You can create the resource group and server ahead of time or while creating the single database itself. You can create a blank database or create a sample database based on Adventure Works LT.

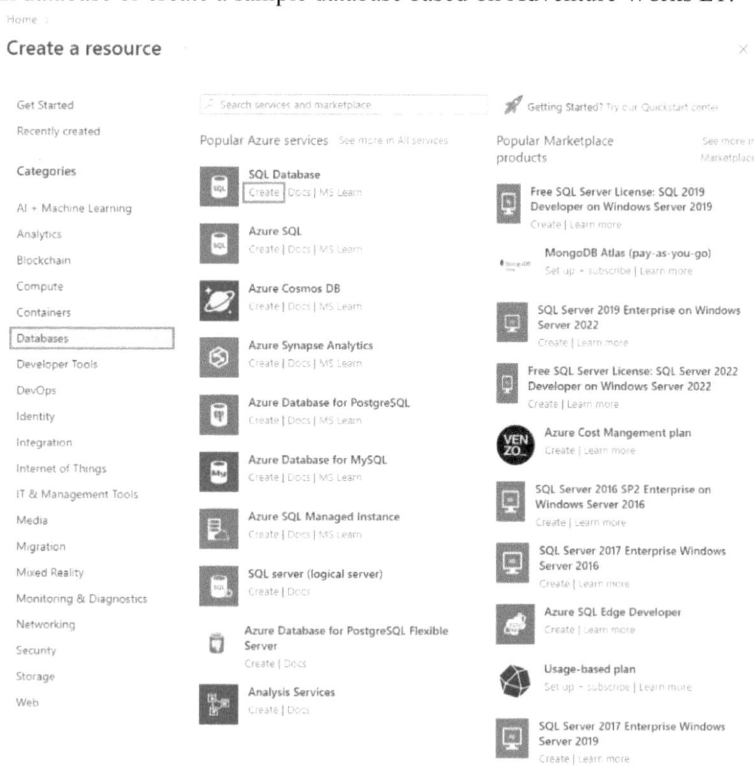

Manage an existing server

To manage an existing server, navigate to the server using several methods - such as from a specific database page, the **SQL servers** page, or the **All-resources** page.

To manage an existing database, navigate to the **SQL databases** page and select the database you wish to manage. The following screenshot shows how to begin setting a server-level firewall for a database from the **Overview** page for a database.

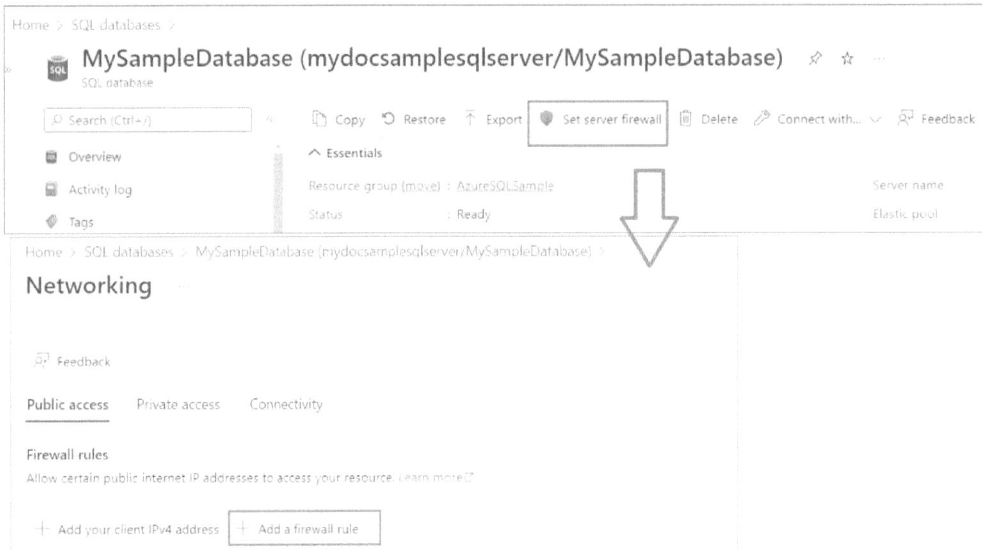

12.4 Scaling and Monitoring in Azure

Scaling and monitoring in Azure are crucial aspects of managing resources efficiently and ensuring optimal performance. Here's an overview of scaling and monitoring in Azure:

Scaling:

Vertical Scaling (Scale Up):

Azure Virtual Machines: Adjust the VM size to a higher SKU with increased resources like CPU, RAM, or storage.

Azure SQL Database: Upgrade the service tier to higher performance levels for increased computing power and storage.

Horizontal Scaling (Scale Out):

Azure Virtual Machines: Use Azure Autoscale or manually increase the number of VM instances to distribute the load.

Azure Kubernetes Service (AKS): Add more pods or nodes to an AKS cluster to handle increased workloads.

Scaling Based on Demand:

Azure Functions: Auto-scale based on demand using serverless computing, ensuring resources are allocated dynamically.

Azure App Service: Configure auto-scaling rules to automatically adjust the number of instances based on load metrics.

Monitoring:

Azure Monitor:

Metrics: Monitor resource usage, performance metrics, and health of Azure services through Azure Monitor.

Alerts: Set up alerts based on defined thresholds to get notified about performance issues or resource utilization spikes.

Logs: Collect, analyze, and visualize logs and telemetry data across applications and resources.

Application Insights:

Application Performance Monitoring (APM): Monitor application performance, detect failures, and track user interactions in real-time.

Dependency Tracking: Trace dependencies across different components of your application.

Azure Cost Management + Billing:

Cost Analysis: Monitor and analyze resource usage and spending to optimize costs.

Budgets and Alerts: Set budgets and receive alerts to manage and control spending.

Azure Advisor:

Recommendations: Get personalized best practices and recommendations for performance optimization, cost reduction, security enhancements, etc.

Security and Compliance Monitoring:

- **Azure Security Center:** Monitor security posture, detect threats, and ensure compliance across Azure resources.
- **Azure Policy:** Enforce organizational standards and compliance by defining policies and monitoring adherence.

By leveraging Azure's scaling capabilities and robust monitoring tools, organizations can efficiently manage resources, ensure optimal performance, and proactively address issues to maintain a healthy cloud environment.

12.5 Exercise

Exercise 1 – MCQ

1. Which of the following best describes Azure SQL Database?
a) An open-source SQL server b) A managed relational database service
c) A NoSQL database solution d) A file storage service
2. What tool is typically used to deploy on-premises databases to Azure SQL Database?
a) SQL Server Management Studio (SSMS) b) Azure Data Studio
c) Visual Studio Code d) SQL Server Integration Services (SSIS)
3. Which Azure service is used for managing and administering Azure SQL Database?
a) Azure DevOps b) Azure Logic Apps
c) Azure Portal d) Azure Active Directory
4. Which option in Azure SQL Database allows you to increase resources temporarily to handle increased workload?
a) Vertical scaling b) Horizontal scaling
c) Automatic scaling d) Manual scaling
5. What Azure tool is used to monitor Azure SQL Database performance and detect potential issues?
a) Azure Monitor b) Azure Data Lake Analytics
c) Azure Stream Analytics d) Azure Data Factory
6. Azure SQL Database is based on which SQL Server technology?
a) Always On b) SQL Server Integration Services
c) SQL Server Analysis Services d) SQL Server Database Engine
7. Which Azure service is used for the deployment of databases to Azure SQL Database?
a) Azure Blob Storage b) Azure SQL Data Warehouse
c) Azure Import/Export Service d) Azure Database Migration Service
8. Which authentication method is commonly used for Azure SQL Database?
a) Windows Authentication b) OAuth Authentication
c) Token-based Authentication d) SQL Authentication
9. Which option allows scaling to a higher service tier automatically in response to workload changes?
a) Elastic Database Pool b) AutoScale
c) Active Geo-Replication d) Dynamic Scalability
10. What feature in Azure SQL Database is used to encrypt sensitive data in motion and at rest?
a) Azure Active Directory b) Transparent Data Encryption (TDE)
c) Azure Key Vault d) Azure Security Center

Exercise 2 – True/ False

1. Azure SQL Database is an on-premises database solution.
2. To deploy a database to Azure SQL, you need to use SQL Server Management Studio (SSMS).
3. Scaling in Azure SQL Database refers only to vertical scaling, not horizontal scaling.
4. Azure SQL Database provides a fully managed service with no need for patching or upgrading.
5. Azure SQL Database allows manual scaling based on performance needs.
6. Azure SQL Database does not offer any monitoring tools for database performance.
7. Azure SQL Database can automatically back up databases and allows point-in-time restores.
8. Azure SQL Database's serverless tier is ideal for constant high-traffic applications.
9. Azure SQL Database does not support geographical replication for disaster recovery.
10. Azure SQL Database is not a part of Microsoft's Azure cloud services.

Exercise 3 – Fill in the blanks

1. Azure SQL Database is a ___________ database as a service solution.
2. To deploy a database to Azure, SQL Server Management Studio (SSMS) is used to perform a _________ to Microsoft Azure SQL Database.

3. When creating a new SQL server in Azure, the user needs to specify the ____________ and ____________.
4. The _____________ feature in Azure SQL Database helps in adjusting database resources according to demand and is cost-efficient.
5. Azure SQL Database provides ___________ and ____________ options for ensuring high availability and disaster recovery.
6. __________ and __________ are important aspects of Azure SQL Database that ensure efficient performance and resource management.
7. The _______________ feature in Azure SQL Database enables users to easily manage and monitor database activities.
8. Azure SQL Database allows scaling based on different _____________, ensuring flexibility and optimal resource utilization.
9. To monitor Azure SQL Database, users can utilize _______________ for tracking database performance and resource utilization.
10. Azure SQL Database offers various _____________ options to suit different application requirements and traffic patterns.

Exercise 4 – One word answer

1. Azure SQL Database Edition for Basic Performance:
2. Azure SQL Database Deployment Tool:
3. Azure SQL Database Monitoring Metric:
4. Azure SQL Database Scaling:
5. Azure SQL Database High Availability Feature:
6. Azure SQL Database Backup Schedule:
7. Azure SQL Database Management Portal:
8. Azure SQL Database Resource Group:
9. Azure SQL Database Performance Monitoring Tool:
10. Azure SQL Database Storage Tier:

Exercise 5 – Small answer

1. What is Azure SQL Database, and how does it differ from traditional SQL Server instances?
2. Describe the key steps involved in deploying an on-premises SQL database to Azure SQL Database.
3. Name two tools commonly used to manage Azure SQL Database, and briefly explain their functionalities.
4. Mention three different service tiers available in Azure SQL Database and briefly explain the differences between them.
5. How does Azure SQL Database handle backup and restore operations? Briefly outline the process.
6. Name two methods available for scaling Azure SQL Database, and briefly describe their purposes.
7. What are the primary aspects of Azure SQL Database that can be monitored, and why is monitoring essential?
8. Provide one example of how you might optimize performance in Azure SQL Database.
9. Name two security features available in Azure SQL Database and briefly explain their significance.
10. How does Azure SQL Database ensure high availability, and why is it crucial in cloud-based databases?

Exercise 6 – Long answer

1. Explain the key features and benefits of Azure SQL Database as a cloud-based database service. Discuss the differences between Azure SQL Database and on-premises SQL Server instances, emphasizing scalability and management aspects.
2. Outline the step-by-step process of deploying an on-premises database to Azure SQL Database. Include details on database migration tools, strategies, and considerations for a successful deployment.
3. Describe the management tasks involved in maintaining an Azure SQL Database. Discuss configuration settings, security measures, backups, and common administrative operations for ensuring optimal performance and reliability.
4. Explain the scalability options available for Azure SQL Database. Discuss horizontal and vertical scaling approaches, and describe how to scale resources up or down based on workload demands.
5. Elaborate on the monitoring capabilities provided by Azure for SQL Database. Discuss tools, metrics, and best practices for monitoring performance, identifying bottlenecks, and troubleshooting issues.
6. Detail the security features and best practices specific to Azure SQL Database. Discuss authentication methods, encryption, role-based access control, and compliance standards implemented in Azure.

7. Explain the automated backup and recovery options available in Azure SQL Database. Discuss retention policies, point-in-time restore, and disaster recovery strategies to ensure data resilience.
8. Describe techniques and optimizations specific to Azure SQL Database for improving performance. Discuss index management, query optimization, and workload isolation strategies in a cloud environment.
9. Discuss high availability features provided by Azure SQL Database. Explain concepts like failover, replication, and geo-replication, outlining their role in ensuring database availability and reliability.
10. Explain strategies for cost management and optimization when using Azure SQL Database. Discuss pricing models, resource utilization monitoring, and recommendations for minimizing costs without compromising performance or reliability.

Answer

Exercise 1:
Answer: 1: C, 2: B, 3: C, 4: A, 5: D, 6: C, 7: D, 8: B, 9: A, 10: B
Exercise 2:
Answer: 1: False, 2: True, 3: False, 4: True, 5: True, 6: False 7: True, 8: False, 9: False, 10: False
Exercise 3:
Answer: 1: managed,2: deploy, 3: firewall, 4: Scaling, monitoring, 5: service, 6: SSMS, 7: performance, scaling, 8: Scaling, 9: replication, 10: configure.
Exercise 4:
Answer: 1: Basic, 2: SSMS (SQL Server Management Studio), 3: DTU (Database Transaction Unit), 4: Elastic, 5: Failover, 6: Automated, 7: Azure Portal, 8: Azure, 9: Azure Monitor, 10: Premium.

ONLINE RESOURCES

Practice Paper
Link: https://forms.office.com/r/6EwRCar23m?origin=lprLink
QR Code:

Chapter 13: Viva/Interview Questions and Answers

Q1: What is the Windows Authentication Mode in SQL Server?
A: This mode connects the server via a Windows account. The server uses the username and password for authentication. In this mode, SQL server authentication is disabled.

Q2: What do you mean by database?
A: A database is a structured form of data storage where data can be retrieved and managed efficiently. It is the collection of tables where the data is stored in an organized way. Tables consist of rows and columns in which rows are also known as records or tuples, and columns are known as attributes. Bank Management Database and University Management Database are a few examples of databases.

Q3: Give an example of a function in an SQL server that returns the first non-null expression from more than one column in arguments.
A: Select COALESCE(sid, sname, marks) from the student;

Q4: Explain the one-to-many relationship in the SQL Server database.
A: When a single column value in one table has a minimum of one dependent column value in some other table, a one-to-many relationship exists.

Q5: What is a Relational Database?
A: A relational database is the collection of data that have an established relationship with each other. It consists of rows and columns. Each row in a database is a record, and columns have the attributes of data. Each row in a table can be identified with a unique ID known as a primary key. And rows in a table can be related to other tables using foreign keys.

Q6: What do you mean by RDBMS?
A: RDBMS is nothing but – Relational DataBase Management System. It is the software that allows storing, managing, querying, and retrieving data from a relational database. And RDBMS interacts with users and the database; it can also carry out administrative tasks such as – managing data storage, accessing data, and assessing database performance.

Q7: Can you differentiate between SQL and MYSQL?
A:

SQL	MySQL
It is the licensed product of Microsoft	It is an open-source platform managed by Oracle Corporation
Knowns as Structured Query Language – It is a query programming language	It is the Relational Database Management System
It uses SQL queries to perform tasks in RDBMS	It has no separate querying language. Uses SQL to perform tasks in RDBMS
Data is protected safely by not allowing third parties to intrude on the SQL servers.	Unlike SQL, it is an open-source platform, so data security wouldn't be as expected.
SQL doesn't support any connectors	MySQL supports connectors such as the workbench tool to build databases.

Q8: What is the significance of CHECK in SQL Server?
A: CHECK constraint limits the values that can be placed inside a table's column. This maintains integrity. The constraint is used column-wise to give specific values to that column. Example: CONSTRAINT CHK_Student CHECK (age<20)

Q9: How to find the 3rd highest marks from the Student table?
A: SELECT TOP 3 marks FROM (SELECT DISTINCT TOP 3 marks FROM student ORDER BY marks DESC) a ORDER BY marks

Q10: What do you mean by Relationships between Tables and mention their Types?
A: Relationships between tables describe how a row in a table is related to a row or rows of another table in a database. There are three types of relationships, as mentioned below:
One to one: When a row in a table has only one related row in another table
One to many: When a row in a table has multiple related rows in another table
Many to many: When a row has multiple related rows in another table and vice-versa.

Q11: What is a trigger?
A: When a table event occurs, such as INSERT, DELETE, or UPDATE, triggers allow executing an SQL code batch. Triggers are managed by DBMS and can also execute stored procedures. [2] For example, when a record is inserted in a database table, a trigger can be set.

Q12: When can records be deleted from a view in SQL Server?
A: Records can be deleted in a 'simple' view as it contains data from one table only.

Q13: What is an Entity in a Database?
A: Entities are nothing but objects that are stored in the master data services models. They are real-world objects that can be distinguishable from other objects. Rows in an entity represent members of the master data, and columns represent attributes of the master data. Generally, entities group the same kind of data. For example, a list of employees of a company.

Q14: What do you mean by Attributes and mention their Types?
A: Attributes are the objects that are included in master data service entities. Also, attribute values are used to describe the members of the entity.
There are three types of attributes, as mentioned below:
Free-form attributes
Domain-based attributes
File attributes

Q15: List down some of the features of MS SQL Server.
A:
It provides an easy and straightforward Syntax.
MS SQL uses transact SQL.
Query optimization is not supported.
The transaction process does not allow rollbacks
Clustering is not supported
Statements are executed serially.

Q16: Which command can be used to get the version of SQL Server?
A: To get the version of SQL Server, use:
Select SERVERPROPERTY('productversion')

Q17: In SQL Server, what is a user defined function?
A: A user defined function allows users to write their logic as per need. The advantage is that it is not limited to pre-defined functions and writing functions, simply complex SQL code. The return type is a table or a scalar value.
Example:

```
Create function sample(@sid int)
  returns table
  as
  return select * from s where Id = @sid
```

Q18: What is SQL Server, and mention its core components?
SQL Server is an RDBMS developed by Microsoft. It has two core components – database engine and SQLOS. The database engine has a relation engine that supports processing queries, and managing database files, pages, indexes, etc. And SQLOS is nothing but a SQL Operating system. SQLOS provides operating systems such as memory and I/O management. It also performs the operations like exception handling and synchronization services.

Q19: Explain types of replications in SQL Server.

There are three types of replications as follows:

Transactional replication- It is a process of data distribution from publisher to subscriber. Transactional replication can be used when data is changed frequently.

Merge replication- It groups the data to a single centralized database from various sources. Merge replication is used in cases where central and branch databases need to update information simultaneously.

Snapshot replication- This replication is the best way to replicate data that changes infrequently, and it is easiest to maintain. Example: Snapshot replication can be used for lists that are updated once per day and needs to be distributed from main server to branch servers.

Q20: Define referential integrity.

Every foreign key value must have a corresponding primary key value. The maintenance of this consistency between foreign and primary keys is known as referential integrity.

Q21: What are TCL Commands? and List down the TCL Commands available on SQL Server?

TCL or Transactional Control Language commands are used to manage different transactions taking place in a database. The three TCL commands are as follows:

Rollback- This is used to restore the database to the last committed state

Save Tran- This saves the transaction, and the transaction can be rolled back to this point.

Commit- Saves the transaction permanently in the database

Q22: Write a SQL Server Query to get the letter 'e' in the name 'Jenna' from the student table.

Select CHARINDEX('e',NAME,0) from student where name='Jenna'

Q23: What is a transaction in SQL Server and mention its modes?

A transaction represents a single task. Once a transaction is over, modifications made in the data will be committed and stored in a database permanently. If an error occurs in the transaction, then the data changes will be canceled immediately.

The following are the modes of transactions:

Autocommit transactions

Explicit transactions

Implicit transactions

Batch-scoped transactions

Q24: What is a Transaction Log, and why is it important?

Transaction log records all transactions and related database modifications of every transaction. To be precise, it records the beginning of a transaction, the changes during the transaction, and the last COMMIT or ROLLBACK of the transaction. The transaction log is one of the vital components in database management since it is used to retrieve the database to a consistent state if there is a system failure.

Q25: As a SQL developer, how will you ensure that SQL server-based applications and databases perform well?

The volume of data, type of information stored, and data to be accessed must be checked. When a system is being upgraded, the present data should be analyzed, and the methods of accessing data should be checked to help understand problem design. Keeping the information about data is necessary when using a new system.

Q26: When should Server-based cursors be used?

When you require to work on one record at any instance of time, instead of taking all the data from the table as bulk. Cursors' performance is affected when large volumes of data are present.

Q27: Tell us about the working of the FLOOR function.

FLOOR function rounds the given non-integer value to the previous least integer—for example, FLOOR(5.6) returns 5

Q28: What do you know about scheduled tasks in SQL Server?

Scheduled jobs or tasks automate processes that can be run at a prescribed time at a regular interval. By scheduling tasks, human intervention is reduced, and tasks can be carried out at any time in the order that the user wants.

Q29: Mention a query that returns the list of triggers in a database.
Select * from sys.objects where type='tr'

Q30: What are ACID properties, and what do they mean?
The ACID properties are nothing but Atomicity, Consistency, Isolation, and Durability. Generally, all transactions must follow ACID properties.
Atomicity: It ensures that a complete transaction must take place in a single execution. Suppose there is only a subset of operations during a transaction, then there could be a compromise in the aim of the transaction. But, atomicity eliminates this possibility.
Consistency: It ensures that a transaction takes place with absolute data consistency before and after the transaction. Simply put, data consistency shouldn't be compromised during transactions.
Isolation: It ensures that each transaction takes place in complete isolation from other transactions. It means that each transaction must run as if it is the only transaction that is happening in the system.
Durability: It makes sure that every transaction must be recoverable when required. Once a transaction is committed, it means that all the data updates have been made in the database then, and they can be retrieved at any time by users.

Q31: Differentiate between rollback and commit.
When COMMIT is executed, all statements between BEGIN and COMMIT become persistent to the database. Whereas, when ROLLBACK is executed, all statements between ROLLBACK and BEGIN are reverted to the state.

Q32: How can you differentiate between a Primary Key and a Unique Key?
The primary key identifies each record in a table. It should have unique values but shouldn't have NULL values. At the same time, the unique key ensures that all the values in a column are different. Simply put, the unique key avoids duplication of data in a column except for NULL Values. Moreover, a table will have only one primary key, but it may have many unique keys.

Q33: How can you relate a Foreign Key and a Primary Key?
A foreign key is a field (s) in a table that links the primary key with another table. A foreign key is mainly used to prevent the loss of a link between two tables. The table that has a primary key is known as the parent table, and a table that has a foreign key is known as the child table. A Foreign key can link with a unique key of another table as it links with a primary key.

Q34: What are Defaults in the SQL Server?
Default is the value specified for a column in a database table. This value will be duplicated in all the new records of the column unless there is no other value specified. In this regard, SQL server management studio is the tool used to specify a default value. Know that we can create defaults only for a current database, and the default value can be truncated when it exceeds the size of the column.

Q35: What are Cursors, and mention their types?
Cursors are known to be the extensions to result in sets that are the group of rows returned for a statement. They help retrieve one or more blocks of rows from the current position. Similarly, they can support data modifications for the rows in the current position in the result set.
There are four cursor types, as you can find below:
Forward only
Static
Keyset
Dynamic

Q36: What are Triggers, and mention their types in the SQL server?
Triggers are the special stored procedures. When there is an event in the SQL server, triggers will run automatically. There are three types of triggers: LOGON, DDL, and DML.
LOGON Triggers: They are fired when a user establishes a LOGON event.
DDL Triggers: They are fired when there is a Data Definition Language (DDL) event.

DML Triggers: They are fired when there is a modification in data due to Data Manipulation Language (DML).

Q37: Explain how to create a table in SQL.
The following query is used to create a SQL table:
Create table name_of_table(column1 datatype, column2 datatype)
For example:

```
create table Student
(
Name varchar(20),
DOB date,
Marks nvarchar(5),
Subject varchar(20)  )
```

Q38: What is the function of a foreign key in a database?
A foreign key is used to define a relationship between the parent and child table connected by columns. The foreign key is a constraint that ensures that the values of the child table appear in the parent table. The foreign key of one table is the primary key of the other, and a table can have several foreign keys. For example:

student {ID, Name, Age, Contact, Gender, Add}
teacher{Teach_ID, Name, ID}

Here, ID is the foreign key for the teacher table.

Q39: What is a Stored Procedure?
It is a function that consists of a group of statements, which can be stored and used repeatedly. Stored procedures can be called and executed as and when required. Stored procedures are stored as 'Named object' in the SQL server database. The result set of the stored procedure depends on the values of the parameters.

Q40: What is the use of an Extended Stored Procedure?
Generally, stored procedures are the blocks of codes that can be accessed by simple application calls. At the same time, extended stored procedures help expand the functionality of SQL servers through external functions written in C or C++ languages. As a result, it allows returning result sets and parameters to the server from different data sources.

Q41: What is a Recursive Stored Procedure?
A stored procedure turns into a recursive stored procedure, including a CALL statement in the procedure body. Here, the CALL statements can be nested. In fact, there is no limit for recursions, but stored procedures nesting is limited by 15 times. Moreover, there are two forms of recursive stored procedures – mutual recursion and chain recursion.

Q42: What is Subquery in SQL Server?
It is known as subquery when a query is nested inside the statements such as SELECT, INSERT, UPDATE, or DELETE. Besides, a nested query inside a subquery is also known as a sub-query. Further, a subquery is also known as an inner query or an inner select. Similarly, the statement that has a subquery is known as an outer query or an outer select.

Q43: What is the importance of views in a database?
There are scenarios where we need to look for a view to getting the solution, such as:
Aggregating data for performance
Customizing the schema and data for a set of users
Controlling access to columns and rows of data

Q44: What are the Types of Subqueries in SQL Server?
The following are the subquery types:
Subqueries with table aliases
Subqueries with IN and NOTIN
Subqueries in UPDATE, DELETE and INSERT statements
Subqueries with comparison statements
Comparison operators modified by ANY, SOME or ALL
Subqueries with EXISTS and NOT EXISTS

ONLINE RESOURCES

Practice Paper
Link: https://forms.gle/moj8yCjaRAyQvTav5
QR Code:

Chapter 14 : Microsoft SQL Server Certificate Practice Questions

1. You have 20 Azure SQL databases provisioned by using the vCore purchasing model.
You plan to create an Azure SQL Database elastic pool and add the 20 databases.
Which three metrics should you use to size the elastic pool to meet the demands of your workload? Each correct answer presents part of the solution.
NOTE: Each correct selection is worth one point.
A. total size of all the databases
B. geo-replication support
C. number of concurrently peaking databases * peak CPU utilization per database
D. maximum number of concurrent sessions for all the databases
E. total number of databases * average CPU utilization per database
Correct Answer: ACE

2. You have an Azure subscription.
You need to deploy an instance of SQL Server on Azure Virtual Machines. The solution must meet the following requirements:
• Custom performance configuration, such as IOPS, capacity, and throughout, must be supported.
• Costs must be minimized.
Which type of disk should you include in the solution?
A. Premium SSD v2
B. Premium SSD
C. Standard SSD
D. Ultra SSD
Answer: A

3. You are designing a multi-tenant enterprise data warehouse using Azure Synapse that holds some crucial data for a Medical and health Insurance company. This data relates to sensitive Protected Health information about patients' ailments and diagnoses.
You need to create a solution to provide Health information management professionals the ability to view all basic entries in patients such as Name, Home Address, and Email.
The solution must avert all Health information management professionals from viewing or inferring demographic information, medical histories, test and laboratory results, mental health conditions, and insurance information.
What should you include to complete this requirement?
A. Data Masking
B. Always Encrypted
C. Transparent Data Encryption
D. Row-level security
Correct Answer : D

4. You have SQL Server 2019 on an Azure virtual machine that contains an SSISDB database.
A recent failure causes the master database to be lost.
You discover that all Microsoft SQL Server integration Services (SSIS) packages fail to run on the virtual machine.
Which four actions should you perform in sequence to resolve the issue? To answer, move the appropriate actions from the list of actions to the answer area and arrange them in the correct.
Select and Place:
Correct Answer:
Step 1: Attach the SSISDB database
Step 2: Turn on the TRUSTWORTHY property and the CLR property
If you are restoring the SSISDB database to an SQL Server instance where the SSISDB catalog was never created, enable common language runtime (clr)
Step 3: Open the master key for the SSISDB database
Restore the master key by this method if you have the original password that was used to create SSISDB. open master key decryption by password = 'LS1Setup!' --'Password used when creating SSISDB'
Alter Master Key Add encryption by Service Master Key

Step 4: Encrypt a copy of the master key by using the service master key

5. You have an on-premises datacenter that contains a 14-TB Microsoft SQL Server database.
You plan to create an Azure SQL managed instance and migrate the on-premises database to the new instance.
Which three service tiers support the SQL managed instance? Each correct answer presents a complete solution.
NOTE: Each correct selection is worth one point.
A. General Purpose Standard
B. Business Critical Memory Optimized Premium
C. General Purpose Premium
D. Business Critical Premium
E. Business Critical Standard
Answer : ABC

6. You have a new Azure SQL database. The database contains a column that stores confidential information.
You need to track each time values from the column are returned in a query. The tracking information must be stored for 365 days from the date the query was executed.
Which three actions should you perform? Each correct answer presents part of the solution.
NOTE: Each correct selection is worth one point.
A. Turn on auditing and write audit logs to an Azure Storage account.
B. Add extended properties to the column.
C. Turn on auditing and write audit logs to an Event Hub
D. Apply sensitivity labels named Highly Confidential to the column.
E. Turn on Azure Defender for SQL

Answer : ADE

7. You have an Azure virtual machine named VM1 on a virtual network named VNet1. Outbound traffic from VM1 to the internet is blocked.
You have an Azure SQL database named SqlDb1 on a logical server named SqlSrv1.
You need to implement connectivity between VM1 and SqlDb1 to meet the following requirements:

- Ensure that all traffic to the public endpoint of SqlSrv1 is blocked.
- Minimize the possibility of VM1 exfiltrating data stored in SqlDb1.

What should you create on VNet1?
A. a VPN gateway
B. a service endpoint
C. a private link
D. an ExpressRoute gateway

Answer : C

8. You have an Azure SQL database that contains a table named factSales. FactSales contains the columns shown in the following table.

FactSales has 6 billion rows and is loaded nightly by using a batch process. You must provide the greatest reduction in space for the database and maximize performance.
Which type of compression provides the greatest space reduction for the database?
A. page compression
B. row compression
C. columnstore compression
D. columnstore archival compression

Correct Answer: D

9. You have a Microsoft SQL Server 2019 database named DB1 that uses the following database-level and instance-level features.

- Clustered columnstore indexes
- Automatic tuning

- Change tracking
- PolyBase

You plan to migrate DB1 to an Azure SQL database.
What feature should be removed or replaced before DB1 can be migrated?
A. Clustered columnstore indexes
B. PolyBase
C. Change tracking
D. Automatic tuning

Correct Answer: B

10. You have a Microsoft SQL Server 2019 instance in an on-premises datacenter. The instance contains a 4-TB database named DB1.
You plan to migrate DB1 to an Azure SQL Database managed instance.
What should you use to minimize downtime and data loss during the migration?
A. distributed availability groups
B. databasc mirroring
C. Always On Availability Group
D. Azure Database Migration Service

Correct Answer: D

11. HOTSPOT -
You have an on-premises Microsoft SQL Server 2016 server named Server1 that contains a database named DB1.
You need to perform an online migration of DB1 to an Azure SQL Database managed instance by using Azure Database Migration Service.
How should you configure the backup of DB1? To answer, select the appropriate options in the answer area.
NOTE: Each correct selection is worth one point.
Hot Area:

Correct Answer:

Box 1: Full and log backups only
Make sure to take every backup on a separate backup media (backup files). Azure Database Migration Service doesn't support backups that are appended to a single backup file. Take full backup and log backups to separate backup files.
Box 2: WITH CHECKSUM -
Azure Database Migration Service uses the backup and restore method to migrate your on-premises databases to SQL Managed Instance. Azure Database
Migration Service only supports backups created using checksum.
Incorrect Answers:
NOINIT Indicates that the backup set is appended to the specified media set, preserving existing backup sets. If a media password is defined for the media set, the password must be supplied. NOINIT is the default.
UNLOAD -
Specifies that the tape is automatically rewound and unloaded when the backup is finished. UNLOAD is the default when a session begins.

12. DRAG DROP -
You have a new Azure SQL database named DB1 on an Azure SQL server named AzSQL1.
The only user who was created is the server administrator.
You need to create a contained database user in DB1 who will use Azure Active Directory (Azure AD) for authentication.
Which three actions should you perform in sequence? To answer, move the appropriate actions from the list of actions to the answer area and arrange them in the correct order.
Select and Place:

Correct Answer:

Step 1: Set up the Active Directory Admin for AzSQL1.
Step 2: Connect to DB1 by using the server administrator.
Sign into your managed instance with an Azure AD login granted with the sysadmin role.
Step 3: Create a user by using the FROM EXTERNAL PROVIDER clause.
FROM EXTERNAL PROVIDER is available for creating server-level Azure AD logins in SQL Database managed instance. Azure AD logins allow database-level
Azure AD principals to be mapped to server-level Azure AD logins. To create an Azure AD user from an Azure AD login use the following syntax:
CREATE USER [AAD_principal] FROM LOGIN [Azure AD login]

13. HOTSPOT -
You have an Azure SQL database that contains a table named Customer. Customer has the columns shown in the following table.

You plan to implement a dynamic data mask for the Customer_Phone column. The mask must meet the following requirements:

- The first six numerals of each customer's phone number must be masked.
- The last four digits of each customer's phone number must be visible.
- Hyphens must be preserved and displayed.

How should you configure the dynamic data mask? To answer, select the appropriate options in the answer area.
Hot Area:

Correct Answer:

Box 1: 0 -
Custom String : Masking method that exposes the first and last letters and adds a custom padding string in the middle. prefix,[padding],suffix
Box 2: xxx-xxx -
Box 3: 5 -

14. DRAG DROP -
You have an Azure SQL database that contains a table named Employees. Employees contains a column named Salary.
You need to encrypt the Salary column. The solution must prevent database administrators from reading the data in the Salary column and must provide the most secure encryption.
Which three actions should you perform in sequence? To answer, move the appropriate actions from the list of actions to the answer area and arrange them in the correct order.
Select and Place:

Correct Answer:

Step 1: Create a column master key
Create a column master key metadata entry before you create a column encryption key metadata entry in the database and before any column in the database can be encrypted using Always Encrypted.
Step 2: Create a column encryption key.
Step 3: Encrypt the Salary column by using the randomized encryption type.
Randomized encryption uses a method that encrypts data in a less predictable manner. Randomized encryption is more secure, but prevents searching, grouping, indexing, and joining on encrypted columns.
Note: A column encryption key metadata object contains one or two encrypted values of a column encryption key that is used to encrypt data in a column. Each value is encrypted using a column master key.
Incorrect Answers:
Deterministic encryption.

Deterministic encryption always generates the same encrypted value for any given plain text value. Using deterministic
encryption allows point lookups, equality joins, grouping and indexing on encrypted columns. However, it may also allow unauthorized users to guess information about encrypted values by examining patterns in the encrypted column, especially if there's a small set of possible encrypted values, such as True/False, or North/South/East/West region.

15. DRAG DROP -

You have a resource group named App1Dev that contains an Azure SQL Database server named DevServer1. DevServer1 contains an Azure SQL database named DB1. The schema and permissions for DB1 are saved in a Microsoft SQL Server Data Tools (SSDT) database project.

You need to populate a new resource group named App1Test with the DB1 database and an Azure SQL Server named TestServer1. The resources in App1Test must have the same configurations as the resources in App1Dev.

Which four actions should you perform in sequence? To answer, move the appropriate actions from the list of actions to the answer area and arrange them in the correct order.

Select and Place:

Correct Answer:

16. You have 40 Azure SQL databases, each for a different customer. All the databases reside on the same Azure SQL Database server.

You need to ensure that each customer can only connect to and access their respective database.

Which two actions should you perform? Each correct answer presents part of the solution.

NOTE: Each correct selection is worth one point.

A. Implement row-level security (RLS).
B. Create users in each database.
C. Configure the database firewall.
D. Configure the server firewall.
E. Create logins in the master database.
F. Implement Always Encrypted.

Correct Answer: BE

17. DRAG DROP -

You have an Azure SQL Database instance named DatabaseA on a server named Server1.

You plan to add a new user named App1 to DatabaseA and grant App1 db_datareader permissions. App1 will use SQL Server Authentication.

You need to create App1. The solution must ensure that App1 can be given access to other databases by using the same credentials.

Which three actions should you perform in sequence? To answer, move the appropriate actions from the list of actions to the answer area and arrange them in the correct order.

Select and Place:

Correct Answer:

Step 1: On the master database, run CREATE LOGIN [App1] WITH PASSWORD = 'p@aaW0rd!'

Logins are server wide login and password pairs, where the login has the same password across all databases. Here is some sample Transact-SQL that creates a login:

CREATE LOGIN readonlylogin WITH password='1231!#ASDF!a';

You must be connected to the master database on SQL Azure with the administrative login (which you get from the SQL Azure portal) to execute the CREATE
LOGIN command.

Step 2: On DatabaseA, run CREATE USER [App1] FROM LOGIN [App1]
Users are created per database and are associated with logins. You must be connected to the database in where you want to create the user. In most cases, this is not the master database. Here is some sample Transact-SQL that creates a user:
CREATE USER readonlyuser FROM LOGIN readonlylogin;
Step 3: On DatabaseA run ALTER ROLE db_datareader ADD Member [App1]
Just creating the user does not give them permissions to the database. You have to grant them access. In the Transact SQL example below the readonlyuser is given read only permissions to the database via the db_datareader role.
EXEC sp_addrolemember 'db_datareader', 'readonlyuser';

18. You have an Azure virtual machine named VM1 on a virtual network named VNet1. Outbound traffic from VM1 to the internet is blocked.
You have an Azure SQL database named SqlDb1 on a logical server named SqlSrv1.
You need to implement connectivity between VM1 and SqlDb1 to meet the following requirements:
- Ensure that VM1 cannot connect to any Azure SQL Server other than SqlSrv1.
- Restrict network connectivity to SqlSrv1.

What should you create on VNet1?
A. a VPN gateways
B. a service endpoint
C. a private link
D. an ExpressRoute gateways

Correct Answer: C

19. You are developing an application that uses Azure Data Lake Storage Gen 2.
You need to recommend a solution to grant permissions to a specific application for a limited time period.
What should you include in the recommendation?
A. role assignments
B. account keys
C. shared access signatures (SAS)
D. Azure Active Directory (Azure AD) identities

Correct Answer: C

20. You are designing an enterprise data warehouse in Azure Synapse Analytics that will contain a table named Customers. Customers will contain credit card information.
You need to recommend a solution to provide salespeople with the ability to view all the entries in Customers. The solution must prevent all the salespeople from viewing or inferring the credit card information.
What should you include in the recommendation?
A. row-level security
B. data masking
C. Always Encrypted
D. column-level security

Correct Answer: B

21. You have a data warehouse in Azure Synapse Analytics.
You need to ensure that the data in the data warehouse is encrypted at rest.
What should you enable?
A. Transparent Data Encryption (TDE)
B. Advanced Data Security for this database
C. Always Encrypted for all columns
D. Secure transfer required

Correct Answer: A

22. You have a dedicated virtual machine that monitors and collects data from SQL Server instance on Azure to investigate performance issues.
The dedicated machine has the following components installed.

- Azure Monitor Agent
- Workload Insights extension

To get started with SQL Insights, from the Monitor blade, we create a profile after selecting SQL (preview).
Name the component we need to configure from "Create profile Page" that would help to send all monitoring data.
A. Monitoring profile
B. Collection settings
C. Log Analytics workspace
D. Azure Activity Log

Correct Answer: C

23. You have an Azure subscription and along with it you have a SQL Server Database which is causing a lot of performance issues.
You have set up an extended events engine in Azure SQL which is a lightweight and powerful monitoring system that allows you to capture granular information about activity in your databases and servers.
Which Channel within the Extended event is typically related to performance?
A. Admin Events
B. Operational Events
C. Analytic Events
D. Debug Events

Correct Answer: C

24. You have a Microsoft Azure Subscription that holds an Azure SQL Managed Instance. This holds tables on various modules of an ERP system. You need to configure automatic tuning on the Azure SQL Managed Instance. Which Automatic tuning option is available for Instance database support?
A. FORCE_LAST_GOOD_PLAN
B. CREATE INDEX
C. DROP INDEX
D. CREATE PRIMARY KEY CONSTRAINT

Correct Answer: A

25. You have a 'server01' running HADR with a primary role and it crashes. The DBA performs a HADR takeover by force on the 'servers02' to switch roles. The 'server02' now becomes the primary server. The below DMVs provide information on the state of a replica. Match the correct definition with their respective DMVs.

	DMV'S		ANSWER AREA
1	sys.dm_hadr_availability_replica_states	A	Returns a row for each Always On availability replica of all Always On availability groups
2	sys.dm_hadr_database_replica_states	B	Returns a row for each local replica and a row for each remote replica in the same Always On availability group
3	sys.dm_hadr_database_replica_cluster_states	C	Returns a row for each database that is participating in an Always On availability group for which the local instance of SQL Server is hosting an availability replica
4	sys.dm_hadr_availability_replica_cluster_states	D	Returns a row containing information intended to provide you with insight into the health of the available databases in the Always On availability groups in each Always On availability group on the Windows Server Failover Clustering cluster

Correct Answer: 1-B, 2-C, 3-D and 4-A

26. You have an Azure SQL server virtual machine.
You need to back up the transaction log from the Primary server instance to the secondary server instance. Which option should you choose?

A.	Implement 'Always On' availability groups
B.	Configure transactional replication
C.	Configure Transaction Log Shipping
D.	Import a DACPAC

Correct Answer: C

27.	You have a large production Azure SQL database named 'bankdb'. You are running a reporting or analytics workload on this data that is causing performance issues.
To overcome this issue you decide to have a second database such that additional workload can be handled thereby minimizing the performance impact on your production workload. Data Sync helps you to keep the two databases synchronized. Below are the steps required to set up SQL Data Sync between databases. Identify the correct sequence from the options below.
A.	Add a Database in Azure SQL Database
B.	Add a SQL Server Database
C.	Create a Sync group
D.	Configure Sync Group
E.	Add Sync Member

Correct Answer: C, E, A, B and D

28.	You have an Azure SQL manage instance that has a database named IBC-data that stores data in geo-redundant storage blobs which are replicated to a paired region. Match the following storage redundancies for backup.
BACKUP STORAGE EDUNDANCIES	ANSWER AREA
Locally redundant storage (LRS)	A	Copying your backups synchronously three times within a single physical location in the primary region using LRS. Then it copies your data asynchronously three times to a single physical location in the paired secondary region.
Zone-redundant storage (ZRS)	B	Copies your backups synchronously across three Azure availability zones in the primary region.
Geo-redundant storage (GRS)	C	Copies your backups synchronously three times within a single physical location in the primary region

Correct Answer: 1-C, 2-B and 3-A

29.	You have a Microsoft Azure SQL database instance running in the single-user mode for a POS application that manages sales and performs day to day operations of the retail store. We have a table named product_specification. The non-cluster index is created on columns
batch_number, name, description, and price. There was a loss of data due to a deadlock caused when multiple users started performing CRUD operations.
Which parameter option under the DBCC(Database Console Commands) check would ensure an integrity check for the given table with no data loss?
A.	NOINDEX
B.	REPAIR_FAST
C.	REPAIR_REBUILD
D.	REPAIR_ALLOW_DATA_LOSS

Correct Answer: C

30.	An instance of Microsoft Azure SQL Server has a Sales Database with multiple objects. You have multiple indexes created on tables. Index pages are increasing massively because of the Insert and Update operation.
Name a stored procedure that provides all information about the fragmentation page and space.
A.	dm_db_index_physical_stats
B.	dm_db_column_store_row_group_physical_stats
C.	dm_db_index_usage_stats
D.	dm_db_index_operational_stats

Correct Answer: A

31. You need to run a Transact-SQL system stored procedure on the Microsoft Azure job agent database. For this, we need to add a new target server member to the target group containing server(s) and exclude a database target member MappingDB from the server target group. Identify the procedure that would help us perform the above tasks.
A. jobs.target_groups
B. jobs.sp_add_target_group
C. jobs.sp_add_target_group_member
D. jobs.target_group_members

Correct Answer: C

32. We have a SQL Server on an Azure VM named CHC-DB-SERVER which holds databases such as RV Medicare, and Medicaid for various clients of an insurance claim company. You add a user as a member of the sysadmin group who would be the SQL Agent operator such that it receives emails as an alert on every job failure. You need to perform certain actions from the below options to achieve the requirement.
A. Create a Job Alert
B. Enable Database Mail
C. Create a Job Notification
D. Enable Email setting for SQL Server Agent
E. Create a targeted Job

Correct Answers: B, D and E

33. You have a Microsoft Azure SQL server virtual machine. You wish to install log shipping such that you could store backups on a dedicated SMTP file share. You need to configure servers to perform the Log Shipping step. Which server instance would you choose to configure and perform actions such as complete backup job & copy backup Job You can choose the same server instance for different actions performed.
A. Monitor Server Instance
B. Primary Server Instance
C. Secondary Server Instance
D. Backup Share file Server

Correct Answers: B and C

34. I want to compress my table dbo.myTable. I start with the following code:
- ALTER TABLE dbo.myTable
- REBUILD PARTITION = ALL
- WITH (DATA_COMPRESSION =

Which of the options is NOT a valid ending to this code?
A. PAGE)
B. ROW)
C. NONE)
D. PREFIX)

Correct Answer: D

35. You plan to create a table in an Azure Synapse Analytics dedicated SQL pool. The data in the table is invoice data under the sales schema for the past 3 years. SQL Monitor has raised a "Long running query" which when executed showed details about all invoices generated over years to gather month-wise sales for individual items. Due to this management decided to purge data, once a year for data that is older than three years.
Using which of the options below can you ensure that data can be distributed evenly across partitions such that the operation of purging data is accelerated?
A. Filegroup
B. Partition scheme
C. Partition Function

D. Partition Column

Correct Answer: C

36. You plan to create a table and you need to establish trust around the integrity of data stored. Ledger provides a chronicle of all alternates made to the database over time. Choose the right option that best defines the ledger table.
A. Implements Row level security
B. Implements Encryption of data.
C. Implements decryption of data
D. Preserves historical data in the history table.

Correct Answer: D

37. London Heathrow Airport is one of the busiest in Europe by passenger traffic. To keep adverse weather, aircraft delays, traffic-clogged highways, public transport slow-downs, and global pandemics from disrupting its operational readiness, and to identify the untapped capacity that it can use to grow sustainably, Heathrow needs an effectively managed data estate. Which Microsoft Azure service would help derive data-driven insights to optimize its operations, support continued growth, and improve air travel experiences.
A. Data Catalog
B. Microsoft Purview
C. Azure Lighthouse
D. Azure CycleCloud

Correct Answer: B

38. We have an Azure SQL Database server named IBC_010122 that stores PHI data for customers at Change health care. This data is accessed and transmitted across networks between the database Server and various HealthTech, and InsurTech Client applications. To encrypt data that is transmitted across networks which form of data encryption is most suitable?
A. Always Encrypted
B. TLS
C. TDE
D. CLE

Correct Answer: B

39. You need to migrate a disk-based table for sales data on a SQL 2014 server to SQL 2016 such that we could have these tables as memory-optimized. A back and restore option was used for this operation. The need for this migration was to improve performance. Determine the Transact-SQL segments you should use such that the performance benefits are concluded and table statistics are updated consequently.

SQL SEGMENTS
A Create procedure sp_inventory
WITH NATIVE COMPILATION
B ALTER DATABASE CURRENT SET
COMPATIBILITY_LEVEL = 130
C EXEC sp_inventory
D UPDATE STATISTICS dbo.sales
E EXEC sp_recompile N' sp_inventory

Correct Answers: B, D and E

40. A company holds a Microsoft cloud subscription. We need to understand how we enable the staff of the company to connect to the cloud services.
We have the Azure virtual network gateway to access the cloud environment.

To ensure a secure connection for all of the users who work at the office, between the data center or office and the Azure virtual network, which of the following VPN option would you choose from below?

A. site to site (S2S) VPN
B. IPSec
C. ExpressRoute
D. point-to-site VPN

Correct Answer: A

41. You have Customer PHI data residing at TIBCO which is a legacy service used to integrate applications using a visual, model-driven development environment by CHC. We need to migrate this data to Azure SQL Database such that we can perform certain analyses.
The TIBCO system produces time series analysis-based reports for customers who are segregated on the basis of aliment diagnosed. There are six ailments on which these analyses would broadly be carried out.
Data from the TIBCO system is stored in Azure Event Hub.
For being affirmative on the diagnosis done for the aliment the reports would be sent to four other departments such that pre-operative assessment and examination tests could be carried out.
Each department has an Azure Web App that displays time series-based assessment and contains a WebJob that processes incoming data from Event Hub.
All Web Apps run on App Service Plans with three instances.
Data throughput must be maximized. Latency must be minimized.
You need to implement the Azure Event Hub. The partition Key is 'department'. What would be the number of partitions required for optimal data distribution?

A. 3
B. 4
C. 6
D. 12

Correct Answer: C

ONLINE RESOURCES

Practice Paper
Link: https://forms.gle/5LHVrsYgYgKCw6R96
QR Code:

ADDITIONAL RESOURCE

Microsoft Access – Quick Introduction: https://youtu.be/oilEviyIOpo

Microsoft SQL Server Playlist
Link: https://www.youtube.com/playlist?list=PLzlh_31VWEFow9PqL3ITYtqvt3JkYojZw
QR Code:

YouTube Videos Playlists for all Chapters

Chapter 1 Playlist Video:
Link:
https://www.youtube.com/playlist?list=PLzlh_31VWEFpnGVgZ2R9XA1_xdhGtxaHY
QR Code:

Chapter 2 Playlist Video:
Link:
https://www.youtube.com/playlist?list=PLzlh_31VWEFpKN1ZtEUrX1QbWA8Jv4aoD
QR Code:

Chapter 3 Playlist Video:
Link: https://www.youtube.com/playlist?list=PLzlh_31VWEFqL2o-gpRbqW1k3KfjTB0Sp
QR Code:

Chapter 4 Playlist Video:
Link:
https://www.youtube.com/playlist?list=PLzlh_31VWEFp6atvnUWZJaUMDHFpIT1id
QR Code:

Chapter 5 Playlist Video:
Link:
https://www.youtube.com/playlist?list=PLzlh_31VWEFpAdlZqYx7VDPHD3k5Q35rY
QR Code:

Chapter 6 Playlist Video:
Link: https://www.youtube.com/playlist?list=PLzlh_31VWEFqQ-9VOv0e2hfNwOnQmZrC1
QR Code:

Chapter 7 Playlist Video:
Link:
https://www.youtube.com/playlist?list=PLzlh_31VWEFo6vc7JfpTLy1MCUYLJX04O
QR Code:

Chapter 8 Playlist Video:

Link: https://www.youtube.com/playlist?list=PLzlh_31VWEFrmbZo7K0Lz188uLLX-cPYm

QR Code:

Chapter 9 Playlist Video:

Link: https://www.youtube.com/playlist?list=PLzlh_31VWEFpj9BH421j3XrcEpIVC-NYA

QR Code:

Chapter 10 Playlist Video:

Link: https://www.youtube.com/playlist?list=PLzlh_31VWEFqeTS41akZLyRfA6hiZPIhO

QR Code:

Chapter 11 Playlist Video:

Link: https://www.youtube.com/playlist?list=PLzlh_31VWEFr29BnAbDI233YdS7ljd-Dn

QR Code:

Chapter 12 Playlist Video:

Link: https://www.youtube.com/playlist?list=PLzlh_31VWEFqTIjqHXsXF6gz0Suer-tyq

QR Code:

Chapter 13 Playlist Video:
Link:
https://www.youtube.com/playlist?list=PLzlh_31VWEFp0uoYi5V8lMxCAA7JcKlOY
QR Code: